Language in Chi

Language in Children provides a concise and basic introduction for students studying child language acquisition for the first time. Starting from the first sounds a child produces, this book covers all the stages a child goes through in acquiring a first language. In ten accessible chapters, this book:

- illustrates developmental stages from the recognition of sounds and words to the ability to hold a conversation, and also covers bilingual upbringing;
- features real-life examples of all the phenomena discussed, from languages such as French, Spanish and Finnish as well as English;
- incorporates guidance on sources for further reading and exploration by chapter;
- is supported by a companion website, which includes links to further material and real-world data on the CHILDES archive.

Written by an experienced researcher and teacher, *Language in Children* is essential reading for students studying this topic for the first time.

Eve V. Clark is Professor of Linguistics and Symbolic Systems at Stanford University, USA.

Routledge Guides to Linguistics

Routledge Guides to Linguistics are a set of concise and accessible guidebooks which provide an overview of the fundamental principles of a subject area in a jargon-free and undaunting format. Designed for students of linguistics who are approaching a particular topic for the first time, or students who are considering studying linguistics and are eager to find out more about it, these books will both introduce the essentials of a subject and provide an ideal springboard for further study.

This series is published in conjunction with the Linguistic Society of America. Founded in 1924 to advance the scientific study of language, the LSA plays a critical role in supporting and disseminating linguistic scholarship both to professional linguists and to the general public.

Series Editor

Betty Birner is a Professor of Linguistics and Cognitive Science in the Department of English at Northern Illinois University.

Titles in this series:

Language in Children
Eve V. Clark

Ebonics
Sonja Lanehart

Why Study Linguistics?
Kristin Denham and Anne Lobeck

Language and Meaning
Betty Birner

More information about this series can be found at www.routledge.com/series/RGL

Language in Children

Eve V. Clark

Routledge
Taylor & Francis Group

LONDON AND NEW YORK

First published 2017
by Routledge
2 Park Square, Milton Park, Abingdon, Oxon OX14 4RN

and by Routledge
711 Third Avenue, New York, NY 10017

Routledge is an imprint of the Taylor & Francis Group, an informa business

British Library Cataloguing-in-Publication Data
A catalogue record for this book is available from the British Library

Library of Congress Cataloging-in-Publication Data
A catalog record for this title has been requested

ISBN: 978-1-138-90604-4 (hbk)
ISBN: 978-1-138-90607-5 (pbk)
ISBN: 978-1-315-53740-5 (ebk)

Typeset in Times New Roman
by Swales & Willis Ltd, Exeter, Devon, UK

Visit the companion website: www.routledge.com/cw/clark

Contents

Preface

In learning to talk, children master a complex system and apply a variety of skills in doing so. This book is intended to offer a first look at what is involved as children acquire a language, how adults talk with them, from a few months old onwards, and how interaction between adult and child plays a critical role in the process of acquisition. Young children attend to expert speakers, talk with them, get feedback from them, and, in interacting, practise what they have acquired so far.

This book gives examples of what children can say at different stages, how they elaborate their utterances as they learn to communicate effectively with language and gesture, establish and accumulate common ground, and add new information when they can to what the other speaker has just said. We know a lot about some of the processes involved, but there are many questions waiting to be asked, and answered, in this field.

My goal in writing this book is to encourage readers to pursue the questions and issues touched on here, find out more about the process of acquisition, and pursue questions about how the amount of social and communicative interaction children have access to affects their acquisition and early use of a language.

EVC
Stanford
January 2016

A few phonetic symbols and their values in English words

Some consonants:

/s/	sit, cats
/z/	zoo, dogs
/ʒ/	azure
/ʃ/	ship, push
/ŋ/	link, monkey

Some vowels:

/æ/	sat, bat
/ə/	schwa/neutral vowel, as in *a* book or *the* book
/ʌ/	but, monkey
/ɪ/	sit, fill
/i/	feel, seal
/ɒ/	hock, dog, cot
/ɔ/	hawk, caught
/ɑ/	father

Nasal vowels are marked with a tilde above the vowel

Notes on age:

Children's ages are reported in years: 2 years old; in years followed by months, as in 2;6 for 2 years 6 months; and in years, months and days, as in 2;6.13, for 2 years, 6 months, and 13 days.

Chapter 1

Where do children learn a first language?

In this chapter, we examine the setting in which children first come to understand and produce language. We'll begin with some general signposts along the way as children begin to master and then become more skilled in using language. We'll also consider, briefly, some of the earlier views of this process, before we turn to some of the general issues we need to address in relation to the process of language acquisition.

Signposts

Very young children show initial comprehension of a few words somewhere around 8 to 10 months, and they typically produce their first words between 11 or 12 and 20 months. Next, they begin to produce longer utterances by combining gestures and words, and then producing two or more words together. This may happen anywhere between 14 and 15 months and 18 and 22 months. (There can be as much as a year's difference in when particular children master a specific feature of language.) Once children begin to combine words, they also start to add word endings like the plural –s in English, and add in small words like *the*, *of*, or *in* as well. Again, learning where and when to use word endings as well as these small grammatical words (often called **function** words) takes time. In some languages, children master these elements in the language by around age 6. In others, some of these details may take them much longer, up to as late as age 10 or 12.

Once children can combine two or more words, they also start to do more complicated things with language. And when they can produce utterances with three or four words, they start using more complex constructions too. For example, they add information to distinguish among the people or objects they are referring to, as in *the **blue** car*, *the man **with the red hat**, the girl **who's running***. They start to talk about sequences of events: *He ran outside **and then** he climbed the hill.* They talk about causal events: *They **made** the boat **capsize**.* They talk about contingent events: ***If** it rains, we'll play inside.* They start to express beliefs and attitudes: ***I think** they like spinach, **He wants** to have a picnic.* And they gradually learn how to do all sorts of things

Age/stage	Comprehension	Production
6–8 months	2–4 frequent words	(early babbling)
9–12 months	10–30 words, frequent routine phrases	babbling, 1–2 words
13–22 months	simple instructions, answer simple questions	10–50 words, word-combinations
2;0–2;6	answer more question types, understand 1000–1500 words	100–600 words, many question types; start to produce more complex constructions
2;6–3;6	increasing skill in turn-taking; further increases in vocabulary size	initiate many interactions, propose new topics, and ratify new information
3;6–5;0	near adult timing in turn-taking; up to 14,000 words by age 6;0	variety of complex constructions, vocabulary of ~6000+ words by age 5; regular addition of new information in own turns; some rudimentary storytelling
5;0+	good comprehension, follow instructions	persuade, give instructions, tell more structured stories, and keep track of characters

Note: Typically a year or more's variance in when a particular child reaches these milestones.

with language, from telling jokes – a favourite at age 5 – to persuading, instructing, managing, and cooperating in all sorts of activities, and also telling more and more elaborate stories.

Some proposals about acquisition

People have long puzzled over how children come to acquire their first language, and a variety of proposals have been made at various times. Here we'll briefly consider a few of these proposals, and why they fail as an adequate account of what goes on as children acquire language. In effect, many proposals that have been made present an unrealistic picture of how acquisition occurs, how long it takes, and the role adults play in it.

One view that arises from behaviourist approaches to psychology is that adults *teach* children their first language. They do this, it is proposed, first by approving of any babbled sounds that belong in the language, but ignoring any sounds that don't belong. Sounds that are accepted, approved of, become shaped into sequences that constitute words. Adults don't reinforce erroneous forms, so even if these were produced, they would be short-lived. The same approach is assumed to work for acquiring words and constructions.

However, parents actually appear to approve of every vocalization – and hence many non-native sounds – produced by babies as they babble. And they typically approve of any attempts to communicate, however defective. Young children start out with many elements 'missing' from their early utterances, and they make certain consistent, and often long-lasting, errors, retaining non-adult-like forms over weeks and even months. In doing this, they seem to be regularizing their language: they make irregular forms regular, as in *sit* with *sitted* as its (regular) past tense, or *mouse* with *mouses* as its (regular) plural form. So it is unclear what role adult approval (reinforcement) or lack of approval actually plays in the process of acquisition.

A related view here is that children simply imitate what they hear around them. But if they learn language by imitating other speakers, why do they begin with just one word at a time, and that only at 12–15 months of age? Why do they take such a long time to put two words together in an utterance? And why do they leave out word endings and small grammatical words like *to*, *of*, and *the* for so long? That is, their early utterances do not seem to be direct imitations of any adult model in their vicinity.

A rather drastic alternative to these views, proposed in the 1960s, was that adults play virtually no role in children's acquisition. They provide no feedback and so never correct errors. Indeed, there is no need in this view for any feedback because the language itself – at least the grammar – is assumed to be innate. At the same time, proponents of this view agree that children do have to learn the sounds of a language, somehow. They also have to learn the vocabulary, which can amount to between 50,000 and 100,000 words by age 20 or so – hence, a massive learning task. But the grammar is there from the beginning, it is claimed, and, in this view, that is what is most important.

Yet children take time to settle on or identify properties central to the grammar of the language they are acquiring, and the process involved in going from innate grammatical categories to possible syntactic constructions in a language has yet to be fleshed out. Moreover, as we will see, adults do offer feedback as part of the conversational to-and-fro as they check up on what their children mean, and they do this for all aspects of the language being acquired. (And we will see how this plays an essential role in the overall process of acquisition.)

Finally, another position often proposed informally is that children learn language when they go to nursery school and kindergarten, hence from their teachers. But children arrive there already talking, often talking rather a lot. So they must already have been working on the early stages of what they need to do to learn a language in their first two or three years. The question is how much they already know by age 3 or 4, and how they got there.

In this book, we will focus instead on the kinds of interactions that adults and babies take part in from birth on, and the critical role these interactions play in the acquisition of language by young children. Children learn their first language from the speakers around them. Initially, these speakers will generally be the adults looking after them. But as infants get older, progress to walking, and start producing single words themselves, they also interact with older siblings and peers as well as caregivers. So it is the ambient language that young children acquire. How does their acquisition take place? Do adults tailor their language for young addressees?

Early adult–child interaction

Adults talk to babies from the start, even though they know that babies can't yet understand any language. Despite this, parents and other caregivers interact with infants, and such interactions, the evidence suggests, are helpful and even crucial for the later acquisition of language. For example, parents rely on mutual gaze, looking at babies, catching their eye; they touch them, hold them, and use affective intonation to communicate comfort, soothing, play, and laughter. Two-way interaction typically begins as soon as small babies respond with smiles and mutual gaze. In these early 'exchanges', with little or no communicative content on the babies' side, adults will treat a smile, a look, a burp, or a leg-kick as a 'turn' in an exchange. But both content and timing here differ from later conversational turns and actual turn-taking with language, with both larger gaps between turns and more overlapping of turns.

Parents engage 2-month-olds with smiles and eye-gaze. From the age of 3 months on, infants can participate with adults in what could be called passive joint engagement where the adult follows the infant's gaze. When infants reach 4 months of age, adults can also get them to attend to objects they show to them. This is also about the time when infants also start watching hand motions intently, and motion in general, and actively track adult eye-gaze during interactions. Around 6–8 months, most infants start to babble, and adults will now expect, even demand, babble-sequences as turns contributed by the infant. By 9–10 months, infants readily participate in a variety of exchange games, passing a toy to and fro with an adult, for example, or alternating roles in bouts of peek-a-boo. It is shortly after this that infants typically attempt to produce their first words.

When infants vocalize, they may simply babble in response to adult comments and questions, but from around 11–12 months, they often combine a vocalization with a gesture, where the vocalization may be based on some adult word, as in uses of a syllable like **da** along with a point gesture at some object of interest. When this happens, adults typically respond with a label for the apparent referent. And once young children begin to label things spontaneously, adults typically confirm any label a child has produced, and then expand on it, as in:

> *Nicola* (1;11.9): *nose.*
> *Mother:*   He's got a pointed nose, hasn't he?

But when children combine a single-word utterance, a label, with a gesture, pointing towards some object, say, or reaching towards something, adults construe this as a request for information or a request with respect to that object, as in:

> *Nicky* (1;7.29): *back, back* <handing plate to Mother>
> *Mother:*   Do you want me to put it back? There.

That is, adults tend to respond differently to children's word-only utterances compared with how they respond to child utterances that contain a word and gesture combined.

Early on, infants' vocalizations often overlap with adult speech: when they smile, when they produce contented cries, and later when they start to babble. But even with a 3-month-old, adults may impose something like turns-at-talk: first making a comment say, then pausing until the infant does something – kicks, yawns, closes its fists, smiles, blinks, or any other action – and only after that do adults resume their talk, taking another turn. Effectively, adult speakers offer a framework for communicative interaction, and even impose it, long before young children actually start to produce any language or participate communicatively, as in the following exchange:

> *Ann* (0;3): <smiles>
> *Mother:* Oh what a nice little smile!
>   Yes, isn't that nice? There.
>   There's a nice little smile.

Ann:	<burps>
Mother:	What a nice wind as well!
	Yes, that's better, isn't it?
	Yes. Yes.
Ann:	<vocalizes>
Mother:	Yes! There's a nice noise.

When adults talk in this way to very young babies, they generally adjust their intonation (the melody of their speech), maybe speak a bit more softly, but don't make any particular adjustments to the content of what they are saying. This content may range from general reflections on the day to talk about activities specific to what the adult is currently doing, e.g. changing or bathing the baby, dressing it, preparing to nurse it. But once very young children display some understanding of a few words, begin trying to communicate with gestures, vocalizations, and even produce a few words (from around 10 months or so onwards), adults start to modify both the form and the content of their speech as they adjust to their addressee's level, taking into account what very young children appear able to understand and what they can produce.

Adults modify their forms of talk

One reason adults adjust their speech as they talk with very young children is to take into account how much infants understand. But adults, sensibly, don't bother to make any adjustments until they see some evidence of comprehension in their children. This typically doesn't happen until around age 10–12 months.

Since children understand so few words at first, adults modify how they talk with young children. They slow down, a lot; they produce very short utterances, they pause between utterances, they use exaggerated intonation contours with a wide pitch range (around two octaves in English speakers, compared to under one octave in talk to other adults), and they wait longer for children to respond, waiting much longer than they would in conversation with an adult. They make these modifications because they are designing their utterances for inexpert, beginning speakers.

Adults also consistently adjust the *forms* of language they use to the child's apparent level of understanding. Besides their exaggerated-sounding intonations, they use higher pitch than in speech to adults; and they produce short utterances, very short compared to when they talk with older children and adults. They articulate what they say clearly; they make very few speech errors – and hence very few repairs to their own speech, and they consistently pause *between* utterances rather than *within* utterances as in adult-to-adult talk. They also readily repeat their utterances, with variations in word order but with much the same content. In short, adult speakers design what they say so it works for addressees who, as yet, know very little about the language or how to use it.

Adults modify the content of their talk

Adults don't just modify the *forms* they use in talking, they also modify the *content* of what they say. When they talk to young children, they do this by choosing their words and their topics. For example, they focus mainly on the here-and-now, offering comments about objects that are physically present and visible to both adult and child, about what is currently happening, about who or what they can both see, and about any changes that are occurring in the scene before their eyes. This focus on the here-and-now places limits on the referents children need to be able to identify when they hear unfamiliar words and expressions. Once they have established joint attention with the adult speaker, their shared focus on the here-and-now helps them 'map' some meaning to unfamiliar word-forms as they identify an unfamiliar referent in context.

Adults attend not only to children's early words but also to their gestures. One-year-olds' pointing gestures are generally taken as an expression of interest or attention, and hence as antecedents to later verbal declarations or assertions. Adults here typically provide a label for the object pointed to, as in the adult 'It's a bear'. But when 1-year-olds instead extend an object towards the adult, adults are likely to take this kind of gesture as a request for help – for instance, help in opening a container with a toy inside, or in winding up a toy, to which adults might respond with 'You want help?' or 'I'll do it'. That is, pointing tends to elicit labels, while reaching towards or extending an object to the adult elicits offers of help and actions that help, from the adult.

In talking with young children, adults repeat themselves a lot. They do this, for example, when they make a request, with slight variations in the form of the request, until they elicit an appropriate response. Such repetitions give children more opportunities – and more time – to work out what is being asked for, and to plan a response. At the same time, of course, the sequence of adult utterances that gets repeated on such occasions serves to display some of the forms that a request can take.

Adult: Pick up the blocks. Put the blocks into the box.
             Put the red blocks away, put them into the box.

Such repetitions also turn up in adults' uses of a label new to the child. In one study, adults offered new labels nearly six times each on average to 1-year-olds, compared to just twice to young 3-year-olds. Adults sometimes rely on 'variation sets', as in the following series of questions designed to prompt the memory of a child aged 2;3 (2 years and 3 months):

Adult: Who did we see when we went out shopping today?
             Who did we see?
             Who did we see in the store?
             Who did we see today?
             When we went out shopping, who did we see?

Such variation sets rely on alternative wording to express the same intention in a variety of ways, substituting different words, and rephrasing questions with additions or deletions, as well as some reordering of information. In one case study of Turkish acquisition, researchers found that variation sets comprised about 20 per cent of the mother's speech to her child between the ages of 1;8 and 2;3. On average, this particular mother produced six variations in a set, with word order varied each time.

Similarly, when parents make requests of their children, they frequently go on repeating the request, in alternative forms, until the children comply. Parents may do this in an attempt to find a version their children understand, or they may do it on the assumption that young children take time to process verbal information (here, a request) so reiterating a request gives them more time to respond.

Parents also frequently repeat forms as a lead-in to elicit information they expect the child to have, generally using test questions rather than true questions, as in:

> *Mother:* Here's the cow. <Mother looks at block>
> Here's the cow. <Mother pushes block towards child>
> What does the cow say? <Mother stops block in front of child>

Adult reliance on repetitions like this seems to be designed to make sure children will eventually work out what the adult wants them to attend to, or to do, on that occasion. Adults also try to get children to produce appropriate information for others and may spend considerable time trying to get them to do this. (We return to this issue later, in Chapter 4.)

Adults scaffold early child contributions

Once children can take turns with single words, adults offer scaffolding or framing to support these turns. They may remind the child of an event ('Do you remember when . . . ?'), and then pause to let the child contribute a relevant word or comment. In doing this, adult and child actively collaborate in recounting the episode. Adult scaffolding or framing supports child contributions, and provides a prompt for the child when adult and child collaborate in retelling a story to someone else. The precise framing given depends on the knowledge of the event that is shared by adult and child.

> *D* (1;6.11, being encouraged to tell Father about episode where Philip, aged 10, let out his budgerigar and it landed on D's head)

Mother:	Did you see Philip's bird? Can you tell Herb?
D:	*head. head. head.*
Mother:	What landed on your head?
D:	*bird.*

When children begin to produce longer utterances and become more skilled at taking turns, adults reduce the amount of framing they offer.

Sophie (3;0):	*why– why do me have to put one slide in?*
Father:	Keep the hair out of your face. Otherwise it's all over you.
	Here. <playing Snakes and Ladders> There's some more counters.
	Will you pass me that green counter?
Sophie:	*which green counter?*

Although adults reduce the amount of scaffolding or framing as their children get older, they continue to expand their children's utterances, not only adding in missing pieces, but also adding information relevant to whatever the child is talking about.

Adults expand their children's utterances

When adults expand on what their children say, adding elements that are missing, they typically add other information too, sometimes in the form of questions, as in:

Brenda (1;7):	/haidi/ [= hiding]
Adult:	Hide? What's hiding?
Brenda:	/brù/ [= balloon]
Adult:	Oh, the balloon. Where? Where is it? Where is it?
Brenda:	/haidiŋ/

Or simply in the form of an expansion on the child's utterance, with the addition of a conventional label for the entity being talked about.

> *Child* (2;3):   *that climbing.*
> *Adult:*   That's for climbing and it's called a ladder.

Expansions like these, along with the rest of what adults say in talk with their children, provide young children with still further exposure to how one conveys specific meanings – the words to use, the grammatical elements and word endings needed, and the ordering of words and any grammatical elements in each utterance.

Adults offer new words

Adults often offer their children words they know their children don't yet know. But they don't just offer new words on their own. They tend to flag words as new by introducing them in frequent fixed frames such as *This is —, That's —, These are called —*. And they often follow up their offers with general information about the referent – about its class membership (the kind of thing it is), about certain parts and properties, relevant functions, ontogeny, and habitat, as in these typical examples:

> • A seal <u>is an animal</u>.   [inclusion in a class]
> • That's a bird, bird <u>with a big beak</u>.   [part]
> • Those are cobblestones. That's a   [property]
>   street <u>made out of stones</u>.
> • That stool is <u>for sitting on</u>.   [function]
> • A lamb <u>is a baby sheep</u>.   [ontogeny]
> • It's called an eel. <u>It lives in the water</u>.   [habitat]

In short, adults not only offer new words, they typically introduce them with a deictic (pointing) expression (<u>*this/that*</u> *is a —*), a deictic combined with *is called* (<u>*these*</u> *are called —*) or a prefatory question like

What is that called? It's a —. And they provide information about the category-type just labelled. This kind of information allows children to relate the meaning of a new word to other words they already know – for instance, other words for animals, toys, foods, vehicles, and, for some 4-year-old enthusiasts, dinosaurs.

It is just such added information that enables children to start constructing semantic domains or semantic fields, sets of words related to each other in meaning. The relation between words can be one of membership or inclusion, as in *That's a ladle. It's a kind of spoon*. It can specify whole and part, usually in that order, as in *That's a rabbit and there's its tail*. Or it can specify some other property, as in *Those guinea pigs have long fur*, or *That ball is made of leather*. The relation can specify function, as in *The wheels make it move*, or *The key is for locking the box*. It can specify habitat, as in *Herons nest in trees*, or *Deer live in the forest*. And it can give information about ontogeny, as in *Horses have foals, cows have calves, sheep have lambs*. Sometimes this information comes in lists of related entities, with the new word given last, as in: *A zebra, an elephant, a monkey, a lion, and a LEOPARD*, or *A spoon, a knife, a ladle, and a WHISK*. Or occasionally adults may give a dictionary-like definition, as in *A picnic is when you eat your lunch outside on the grass*.

Another source of information about semantic fields and semantic relations among words is where certain kinds of talk occur. Adults use some words much more often in some physical locations than in others. Inside a house, for example, they use words for kinds of food, for cooking, and for utensils and pans, with greater frequency in the kitchen than in any other rooms. In the bathroom, they make frequent use of words related to having a bath (e.g. *tap/faucet, water, spray, soap, toy duck, flannel/face-cloth, clean, dirty*), and in the bedroom, terms for morning and evening routines that involve waking, dressing, terms for clothing, pyjamas, covers, sleeping, and so on. And in the front hall, they talk about outdoor clothes (e.g. *coat, shoes, boots, scarf, mittens,* and *hat*). The words adults offer, in short, are relevant to the customary activities associated with particular places and routines. The added information adults provide relates word meanings to each other, and helps children organize their growing vocabularies into semantic domains. The added information also links words across domains. This helps children establish not only what a new word can refer to in the world, but also what its meaning or sense is. (We return to the reference-sense distinction in Chapters 3 and 4.)

Adults provide feedback

By talking with children, adults offer them opportunities both to *discover* the forms of language and to hear how these are *used* for communication. Adults also contribute feedback on what their children say, and how they say it, along with opportunities for practice in using language. Adult feedback takes several forms. It may consist of offering children the right words to use in context, telling them, for example, how to ask for a toy from an older child, or how to greet a relative. In other cases, it may focus on their own understanding of exactly what their children intended to say: that is, they check up on what children mean to say when they make errors.

These errors could be mistakes in pronunciation, which can obscure the target words intended; mistakes in the shapes of words and their endings (in their morphology), as when children produce a present-tense verb (e.g. *bring*) in lieu of its past-tense form (*brought*), or a singular verb form (*he runs*) in place of a plural one (*they run*); mistakes in word-choice (e.g. calling a lighthouse a *farm*), or mistakes in the syntactic construction (e.g. *those fall down from me*). When children make such errors, adults typically check up on what they mean by initiating a side sequence, where they query what the child means by using a conventionally worded utterance with rising intonation, as in:

> *Ben* (1;11.25):   *hat.*
> *Mother:*   She has a hat on?

And children often take up the 'corrected version' in their next turn, as they accept the adult interpretation or clarify their meaning, as in:

> *Child* (1;11):   *play that.*
> *Mother:*   You're going to play with that?
> *Child:*   *Mummy, you play that.*

On occasion, the child's intended meaning may take more negotiation and require several turns to establish, as in:

Abe (2;5.7)*:*   *the plant didn't cried.*
  || *Father:*   the plant cried?
  || *Abe:*   no.
Father: Oh. the plant didn't cry
Abe: *uh-huh.*

On other occasions, adults may use an embedded correction, where they replace the child error in word-form or word-choice with a conventional adult form, again as they check, with rising intonation, on whether this was the meaning the child intended, as in:

Philippe (2;1.26): *les mettre dans le garage* 'put them in the garage'

Adult: Il faut les mettre dans le   'You have to put them in the
  garage?   garage?'

Philippe: **faut** *les mettre dans le garage.*   'have to put them in the garage'

Or adults may simply offer implicit corrections – and conventional labels – in their next utterance, as in:

Mother: And do you know what this is? <points at page>
Christina (1;7.7): /dʌt/ [= cat] <child then points at page too>
Mother: That's another cat. But that's a different kind of cat.
                  It's a cub. It's a baby lion.

And children often take up some or all of the conventional forms offered this way, as in Abe's uptake of the phrase *on it*:

Abe (2;5.10)*:*   *I want butter mine.*
Father: OK give it here and I'll put butter on it.
Abe: *I need butter **on it.***

This kind of feedback is quite extensive, with adults following up between 40 per cent and 60 per cent of child errors up to around age 3;6, in middle- and upper-class speakers of English and French. The reformulations adults offer are the outcome of their checking on just what their children meant, something that is often obscured when children make errors in what they say. However, adult feedback does not necessarily take the same form across social classes within a culture, or across cultures. Differences in child-rearing practices have a major influence on the forms of adult feedback actually offered in communicative interactions.

In many societies, including the K'iché Maya, adults do not rely on high pitch or exaggerated intonation contours in speaking to young children. This is because high pitch marks respect and is used for addressing high-status adults. But pitch can play a slightly different role in marking a special child-relevant register, as in Papua New Guinea, where Kaluli-speaking adults often 'speak for the child', using a special high nasal melody. So until there are more data on the options for offering feedback in different cultures and social settings, we cannot assume that any particular form of feedback is universal. What does seem to be general is that children do receive feedback on their usage in some form during the period when they are acquiring a first language.

Adults ask children questions

Adults continually ask young children questions. Many of these are *yes/no* questions. These amount to around 40 per cent of questions asked before age 3;6. *Yes/no* questions are easier to answer than *Wh* questions, since the addressee has only to agree or disagree with their content. *Wh* questions pose a harder problem because children have to come up with an answer themselves. In answering a *What* question, they need to retrieve the appropriate label from memory (if they know it); for a *Where* question, they need to recall the location of the object being sought. And in each case, they need time to formulate an answer. Adults start out asking only *What* and *Where* questions, typically about objects in the here-and-now, so these are often not yet true questions.

Adults generally use *What* questions to elicit object labels from children, and their frequent *Where* questions, for example, in such settings as the identify-a-body-part routine: 'Where's your nose?', 'Where's your mouth?', 'Where're your toes?', etc. Only later do *What* and *Where* questions become true information-seeking questions. At age 2 or so, children display little or no comprehension of questions beginning with *Who, Which, Why,* or *When*. Adults add these other *Wh* question types as children get older and become more consistent in giving evidence that they understand a specific question type by answering appropriately. Not surprisingly, adults tend to ask only the kinds of questions their children can answer, but they start asking harder questions as soon as children display more comprehension and begin to make use of more elaborate utterances.

Joint attention, physical co-presence, and conversational co-presence

Adults tend to talk with young children about the here-and-now. They label nearby visible objects and actions; they describe the properties and functions of those objects; and they comment on events they are currently involved in. One issue for young children is how to identify the intended referents in such talk. The solution, it seems, is that adults talk about what is *in joint attention*, what is being attended to by both adult and child on that occasion. Adults establish joint attention with children either by following in on what their children are already attending to, or by attracting and then holding their children's attention on some object or event. What is in that shared locus of attention, then, provides the most likely referent or referents for any adult referring expressions (e.g. *that dog, the tree over there, your cup*) produced on that occasion. This helps children 'solve' the relation of word form and word meaning (this is called the mapping problem) as they begin to attach meanings to unfamiliar words. (We will return to this mapping problem in Chapter 3.)

In talking about the here-and-now, adults focus primarily on whatever is *physically* present in joint attention. And they make use, where possible, of terms already familiar to their children along with any new words. Familiar words help children build on their knowledge of what any unfamiliar words might mean on those occasions, in those contexts. In doing this, adults rely not only on language but on gaze, gestures, stance, and general orientation to the entity or activity being talked about. In labelling instances of new categories unfamiliar to the child, they typically point at the object as they label it. And, for example, they offer labels for whole objects before they attempt to label parts of those objects or offer connecting links to other words.

Summary

Adults adjust how they talk to children, with their adjustments tailored to what children can understand and say. This is particularly useful for young children who have to master the sound system of the language, and so learn to get the pronunciation of their words right. Children also have to build up a vocabulary for talking about the objects and events around them. They have to add the right word endings (part of the morphology of the language) along with any small grammatical words like *the*, *of*, or *in*, to the words they produce, and they have to choose appropriate constructions (the syntactic options in the language).

Adults adjust both the form and content of their utterances, and the adjustments they make change as children show they understand and begin to produce more language. Adults don't make such adjustments only for young children: they adjust how they say things for all their addressees. They take account of common ground (based on prior conversations and interactions); they take account of the current perspective on an event (reflected in their choice of words: *the dog* versus *that animal*, *the cars* versus *the polluters*), and they attend to existing referential pacts, to what they have called that object on previous occasions when talking to that addressee. With young children, adults are dealing with beginning-speakers who, as yet, know very little language, and therefore need more expert adult speakers to take into account their state of development and general knowledge as they talk with them.

Adults also check up on what their children intended to say, especially when children make errors in how they say things. This checking-up in middle- and upper-class Western communities takes the form of a reformulation of what the child apparently wanted to say, but the adult version is conventional and grammatically complete, and so offers the child a possible model, provided the adult got the intention right. Children respond to reformulations by repeating some or all of what was 'corrected', by acknowledging the adult's interpretation with *uh-huh*, *mm*, or *yeah*, or by forging ahead with the next turn – thereby tacitly accepting the adult's interpretation. This kind of feedback plays an important role in offering children an immediately contrasting version right after they have made some kind of error. It adds targeted information about the language being acquired, information tailored to the child's immediately preceding utterance.

Chapter 2

Recognizing and producing words

To acquire and use language, children need to recognize the words they hear, so they can retrieve any meanings they have already linked to those words. And they also need to be able to retrieve from memory and then produce words to express their own intentions. To do this, children must store words in memory, along with any information accrued so far about the meaning and use of those words. Any forms stored in memory will be invaluable for recognizing and understanding what another speaker has said. How do children manage this? When do they begin to recognize sequences of sounds, or words? What must they store in memory in order to recognize a sequence of sounds or a word? And how readily can they retrieve such information from memory when they want to produce a word?

Children need exposure to the sounds and sound-sequences that make up words before they can store them for recognition. They also need practice before they reach the same speed in word-recognition as adults. But once they begin to store words and sound-sequences in memory, these offer children a model of what those words should sound like, a model they can use whenever they try to say them for themselves. Producing words correctly takes extensive practice and, at the beginning, young children often fail to produce words that are recognizable to others.

Children therefore rely on their representations of words in memory for both comprehension and production. That is, they set up representations in memory for the words they have identified in the speech around them, so they can recognize those words when they hear them again. Children add to this memory store every day as they encounter new words, assign preliminary meanings, and add them to their current repertoire. And the same representations offer them a model or template for what their own productions of those words should sound like.

How early do infants extract words from the 'speech stream'? When do they first identify a sequence of sounds as a word? In this chapter, we first review the antecedents to infants' identification of words, namely their early-emerging ability to distinguish differences between sounds in their first few months of life. This step eventually allows them to extract recurring sequences of sounds, aka words, from the speech stream. Later, children come to recognize sequences of sounds and distinguish familiar sequences they have heard before, from new, unfamiliar ones. They next pay increased attention to the sounds of the ambient language, and provide the earliest evidence of word recognition. We review these stages before considering word recognition on the one hand, and evidence that young children store adult-like word forms for use in word recognition, and also, less directly, for word production, on the other.

Perceiving sounds

Children attend to human voices from the start: they can localize speech sounds from birth on; after birth, they attend more to the ambient speech heard previously in the womb, in filtered form (think about hearing speech under water), than to speech from another language never heard before, filtered or not. In fact, babies begin to discriminate differences between speech sounds by the age of 2 months. How can we tell? When babies are given a pressure-sensitive, blind nipple to suck on, they suck harder when exposed to a new sound (or when they see a new picture). But as they get used to the sound being played, they suck more and more slowly. Then, if the sound they are hearing changes, from **ba** to **da** say, their sucking on the pressure-sensitive nipple speeds up again. Using sucking rate as a measure allows researchers to tell whether babies discriminate a difference between **b** and **d** in the syllables **ba** and **da**. If they don't detect a difference, their sucking rate just tails off even when they are exposed to a new sound; but if they detect a difference, they show this with consistent increases in sucking rate.

Detecting a difference between speech sounds turns out to be **categorical**. When adults or infants hear synthetic speech sounds that change incrementally through a number of steps on a continuum from **ba** to **da**, they perceive a difference between the two at some point. For part of the continuum, they hear the target syllable as beginning with **b**; after that point, they hear it as beginning with **d**. In short, infants' perception of regular shifts along a dimension is actually categorical, with the continuum divided into two, for syllables beginning with **b** versus **d**. Categorical perception is not unique to humans: it turns up in chinchillas too, and also in quails, so it appears to be integral to how the ear works.

Discrimination of differences, though, is not the same as recognition of the sounds or sequences of sound involved. Getting to recognition takes longer. Between 2 and 10 months of age, infants show categorical detection of differences for stop consonants like **b**, **d**, and **g** (sounds pronounced at the lips, at the ridge just behind the teeth, and still further back against the hard palate in the mouth); differences in voicing (voicing is vibration of the glottis (feel your Adam's apple)) like **b** versus **p**, **g** versus **k**; differences in place of articulation like alveolar **d** (with the tongue against the ridge behind the teeth) versus palatal **k** (with the tongue against the back of hard palate); differences between liquids like **l** versus **r**; nasals like **m** versus **n**; fricatives like **s** versus **z** (the latter is voiced), and for vowels like **a** versus **i.**

Discrimination and attention

Infants are also good at discriminating between sounds that do not occur in the ambient speech they are exposed to. For example, children with ambient English are also good at discriminating the Hindi alveolar **t** from retroflex **t** (with the tongue tip against the hard palate). But this ability appears to fade around 10 months of age. At this point, they start to attend more closely to the sounds in the ambient language, and to ignore sounds from other languages.

According to some researchers, children's earlier discriminatory ability is simply lost at this point in development, but according to others, the loss is more likely an outcome of selective attention. Children attend more to contrasts in the ambient language as they start to store more sequences of sounds extracted from the language they hear. This effect of attention appears to offer the most plausible explanation because children clearly recover their ability to discriminate among non-native sound categories – for instance, when they acquire a second language in childhood and become bilingual. When this occurs early enough, they can discriminate the sounds in their next language just as well as they do those in their first language.

Infants don't attend only to differences in single sounds. By 8 months or so, they also attend to sequences of sounds and show some recognition for sequences they had heard briefly before, compared to unfamiliar sequences. Studies have also shown that from 8 or 9 months on, some infants recognize a small number of words, often words they have heard frequently in routines and formulaic utterances. Adults tend to say the same thing every time they change a nappy or diaper (*Here we go*), every time they put on a child's T-shirt (*Up with your arms*), every time they lift the child into a high chair (*Upsy-daisy*), every time they give the child a bath (*In you get*), and so on.

Some frequently used daily routines

Bedtime: In you get, Tuck you in, Night-night, Lights out
Dressing: On with your pants!, Now the first sock, On with your shoes!
Diaper/nappy changes: Just lie still, All clean, Let me do you up
Mealtimes: Another spoonful, One more bite, Finish your juice . . .
Going upstairs: One, two, three, four . . .
Going outside: Find your mittens, Let's put on your hat, On with your boots
Story-time: Look at that!, Now turn the page, What do you see here?, What's that?
Exchange games: Now you take it, Give it to me, Peek-a-boo

Recognizing words

Word recognition, though, requires added processing: infants, young children, and adults all depend on some representation of each word to have been stored in memory. Within any one language, infants and young children are faced with variation in how each speaker produces specific words, from one occasion to the next. Each utterance of a word like *milk* or *lunch* can differ slightly, depending first on the individual speaker, then also on its syntactic context (the words surrounding *milk*, say, e.g. *That milk's sour* versus *She wants some milk*), the speaker's rate of speech (how fast or slow), who the addressee is (young or old, familiar or a stranger), the addressee's age (small child versus a teenager versus another adult), and so on. So the representation of each word in memory must be flexible enough to take into account individual variations in pronunciation, along with variations contributed by different speakers, speaking with different degrees of formality.

The speech registers or styles that speakers use may range from very informal (casual, fast speech to family and friends, say) to very formal (slower, more careful, speech in settings with strangers). There can also be extensive variation across speakers. This is obvious in speakers of different dialects, signalling social class and/or geographic region. The same speaker may control two major varieties of a language, a local one (a dialect) and a standard version (the standard dialect used in schools, say, and for all non-local transactions), with speakers' choices depending on the addressee and the occasion. Children who are exposed to both from the start need to be able to recognize different versions of words as 'the same', for example, whether *dog* is pronounced as /dɒg/ or as /dɑg/, or *hawk* as /hɔk/ or /hɒk/. Evidence that early word-representations are based on adult pronunciations of words comes from two sources. First, children readily identify conventional adult pronunciations from strange speakers, and second, they recognize conventional versions of words faster than distorted versions of the same words, even when the latter remain quite recognizable.

Young children begin to show some skill in dealing with variations in how words are pronounced as early as 12 months, and soon after this show they can deal with different dialects as well. By age 2, some young children also quickly accommodate to a foreign accent as well.

Overall, children become rather efficient at recognizing words during their second year. They look towards a target picture in a forced choice setting (where they have to choose one of two pictures) more quickly when they hear a word that refers to just one of them. At 1;3, their mean response time in looking to the target is 1,000 milliseconds (one second), but by 2;1, they take just under 800 milliseconds. In short, they speed up steadily in recognizing words, and by 2;6 to 3;0, they are getting fairly close to adult speed.

The evidence that young children store words in memory early on comes from several sources. First, they recognize more and more words, as shown by their responses to what the adult says. For example, they look at or fetch a specific toy or item of clothing when they hear the relevant label, even without fully understanding the adult's utterance, as in:

Father asks small son: Do you need a dry diaper?
Child leaves room and comes back with a (clean) diaper.
Father changes him, and says: There, now you have a dry diaper.
Child left the room again and came back with another diaper . . .

As they get older, they follow up earlier adult utterances appropriately, and so display more understanding of what the other person just said, as in:

Shem (2;8, looking at the UV meter on the tape recorder)
Adult: That's recording the sounds. When you make a sound it moves.
Shem: *dat, dat makes da TALK-sound.*
Adult: The what? That clock-sound?
Shem: *no, no, no, da TALK.*
Adult: The talk-sound? Yeah. Right.

When examined more closely, it becomes clear that what children store in memory is based on the adult word-forms they hear, rather than the (often incomplete) forms they can produce themselves. They need the adult-like word-forms, of course, to recognize the words when they hear them from adult speakers. This suggests that they set up adult-like representations in memory, based on adult versions of words, but these representations must be flexible enough to work for the same speaker on different occasions, for different speakers, and for different dialects. That is, children need to be able to recognize different renditions of, say, *car*, or *book*, or *copycat*, and successfully identify these words on each occasion – from different speakers, in different contexts, in different dialects, and even in different foreign accents.

Adult forms versus child forms

Why do children need to distinguish adult and child versions of a word? They need to be able to do this in order to get better at producing words themselves. Indeed, they consistently prefer adult versions of words to their own. And they are aware that they cannot (yet) say certain words in an adult way. This indicates that they detect the mismatch between their (adult-like) representation of a word and their own production, as in:

Father:	Say 'jump'.
Amahl (2;2):	*dup.*
Father:	No, 'jump'.
Amahl:	*dup.*
Father:	No, 'jummmp'.
Amahl:	*only Daddy can say **dup**!*

When they hear a word, they access the adult form even when they can't produce it themselves. Amahl also consistently produced /sɪp/ for both adult noun *ship* and the verb *sip*. But upon hearing an adult say *sip*, he always took it to be the verb, meaning 'drink a little bit'. Similarly, he produced /maus/ for both adult *mouth* and *mouse*. But when asked to get pictures of one or the other from another room, he always reliably distinguished the two, and returned with the right picture.

This general phenomenon, where the child prefers the adult pronunciation over his own imperfect one, has become known as the *fis* phenomenon:

One of us, for instance, spoke to a child who called his inflated plastic fish a *fis*. In imitation of the child's pronunciation, the observer said: 'This is your *fis*?' 'No,' said the child, 'my *fis*.' He continued to reject the adult's pronunciation until he was told, 'This is your fish.' 'Yes,' he said, 'my *fis*.'

Children rely on their representations of adult word forms in identifying words they hear from others. On occasion this can make for misunderstandings, as when two children, and the adult talking to them, fail to identify the target of *grue* as *glue*, and then go on to mistake the child form *glow* as *grow* (instead of another attempt by the same child at producing *glue*):

Jack (3;4.22, talking about wires getting cut and how to glue them back):	*but if you cut it you have to* **grue** *it back together. that would be difficult.*
Adult:	That would be hard, yeah.
Jack:	*and you have to just* **glow, glow, glow.** (another attempt at 'glue')
Ophelia (4;2):	*but it cannot* **glow** *back together.* (accessing adult 'glow')
Teacher:	I don't think wires <u>grow</u> back together. (interpreting 'glow' as 'grow')

Further compelling evidence for the /fɪs/ phenomenon comes from an experiment with 3-year-olds who were asked to name all the objects on a large sheet of pictures. They then listened to their own versions of each label, the versions produced by another 3-year-old, and the versions produced by an unfamiliar adult. They recognized their own productions only 48 per cent of the time, and those of another 3-year-old 52 per cent of the time. But they correctly identified the words said by the unfamiliar adult 94 per cent of the time. The probability of recognizing a word increased if it was produced with (a) the right initial sound, (b) the right number of syllables, and (c) the right stress pattern. The results here are best explained by the children's having stored adult-like versions of the target words in memory. This would enable them to recognize the words produced by a strange adult, while accounting for why they fail to recognize their own productions or those of their peers when those departed from adult-like pronunciations.

Unanalysed chunks

Children store more than single words in memory. They store some larger chunks too, especially chunks based on phrases that recur frequently in adult – and child – speech. For example, one often hears /wɒtsæt/ for 'what's that'; /weəz/ for 'where is'; /ætsə/ for 'that's a', /lɛsgowautsai/ for 'let's go outside'; or /smaitɜn/ for 'it's my turn', and so on, prior to any analysis and identification by the child of the smaller units that make up such formulaic phrases. Phrases like these may remain as fixed forms for children for many months. Their recourse to such formulaic sequences may even help them identify irregular forms. For example, 4-year-olds consistently produce the form *mice* when prompted with the fixed phrase *Three blind mice* – at a stage when they produce the plural of *mouse* otherwise as *mouses*.

The point here is that children do not analyse all phrases into their constituent parts right away. Such analyses can take time, and children often grasp the speaker's goal in using a phrase or routine utterance from the contexts it is used in and so are able to make some use of it before they understand it in detail. But they start to offer spontaneous analyses of words and phrases from around age 2, relating certain parts of complex words, for instance, to other words they already know, as in:

(a) Child (2;4.3, looking at a toy car): *that a motor car. it got a motor.*
(b) Child (2;6): *does a butterfly . . . make butter?*
(c) Child (2;9.10) *you know why this is a high chair? because it is high.*
(d) Child (2;9.24, at the airport): *you know what you do on runways? you run on them because they start with 'run'.*

Producing words early on

In early production, children fare much less well than in early comprehension. They have great difficulty at first in producing words so they are recognizable to others. The production of sounds requires fine motor control in the articulatory tract – the lips, tongue, jaw, hard palate, velum, so as to keep distinct all the sounds that contrast in that language. And some sounds are harder to produce than others: liquids like **r** and **l**, voiced stops at the ends of words, like the **–g** in *dog* or the **–d** in *bed*, and the combinations of sounds in consonant clusters like **st–** in *stop* or **–mp** in *jump*. To articulate each word so it is recognizable, children must hone their fine motor skills for producing language. This takes time and, above all, practice.

Children's earliest words are typically far from the adult versions they have as their targets. These early pronunciations often take the form of simple Consonant + Vowel (CV) combinations, as in the one-syllable /bɑ/ for 'bottle' or /dɑ/ for 'that'. Young children are more likely to manage an appropriate initial consonant in early words, usually voiced, as in /di/ for 'tree', with an initial voiced **d–** in lieu of voiceless **t–**, but they have a hard time producing final consonants, especially when these are voiced, as in *bib*, *red*, or *frog*. They usually omit these final sounds altogether, as in /rɛ/ for 'red'; or they may produce them in devoiced form, as in /bɪp/ for 'bib'; or, in some cases, they produce words like this with a final nasal sound followed by a devoiced stop, as in /fʷɒŋk/ for 'frog'. In short, they produce versions that seem to be easier, using sounds they have already mastered in final position.

Many early words take a CV form (sometimes reduplicated to CVCV) or CVC, regardless of how long the adult target is. Children may initially produce adult *ball*, *bottle*, and *button* all as /bɑ/. While the adult forms here all begin with **b**, some child productions may be hard to link to the relevant adult target without enough context. For example, one 18-month-old produced the adult word *squirrel* as /gɑ/. How this happened can be captured in the following set of actions:

Squirrel, phonetically /skwɪrəl/

(a) Simplify the initial consonant cluster:
     drop the fricative /s/ and the glide /w/, leaving /k/
(b) Voice the initial stop: /k–/ → /g–/

(continued)

(continued)

(c)   Drop the liquids /r/ and /l/ (too hard to say)
(d)   Go for the maximal vowel, with an open vocal tract,
       changing /ɪ/ → /ɑ/

   •   Outcome for production: /gɑ/

As children get better at articulating one-syllable words, they some-times adopt temporary 'templates' for more complex (multi-syllabic) word forms and use them for any words that happen to fit the template. These templates generally seem to be linked to particular sounds or sound combinations in the target words. For example, the words *blanket, monkey,* and *slinky* were grouped together by one child, apparently on the basis of the medial **–k–** sound, with reduplication of the first segment (the first sound) plus a vowel, so for some weeks, these words were produced as /babɪk/ for 'blanket', /mʌmɪk/ for 'monkey, and /lɪlɪk/ for 'slinky', respectively. 'Blanket' and 'slinky' next became /bakɪt/ and /lɪlɪŋk/, and then, after several more weeks, were produced in near-adult form as /baŋkɪt/ for 'blanket' (only miss-ing the **l** after the initial **b–**), adult-like /mʌŋkɪ/ 'monkey', and /lɪŋkɪ/ 'slinky' (missing the initial **s–**). This child's goal, in all this, was two-fold: produce the words in (a) a consistent form and (b) in a form that others can recognize.

Practice

Children need practice in order to produce recognizable words. And practise they do, commenting to themselves on their ongoing play and rehearsing daytime episodes at bedtime. And of course, they practise extensively as they interact with the people around them, trying to make their own intentions clear, and responding to others' comments and requests for information.

When they practise, they practise sounds, as in Antony's bedtime monologues at age 2 (the slashes separate each utterance in his practice sequences of utterances):

- back *please* / berries / *not* barries / barries ba barries barries / *not* barries / berries / ba ba

Anthony also practised building up and breaking down phrases, as in:

- block / yellow block / look at the yellow block light / see yellow blanket / up there in yellow light
- Anthony jump out again / Anthony jump another big bottle / big bottle

And he practised various grammatical patterns, as in:

- what color / what color blanket / what color mop / what color glass
- I go up there / I go up there / I go / she go up there
- put on a blanket / white blanket / and yellow blanket / where's yellow blanket

They gain further practice when they are playing. For example, in commenting on their own play, children try out variations in wording and word order. They describe what is happening as they set up different scenarios and adventures for dolls, smurfs, action figures, farm animals, or car collections. They comment on their own actions in solitary play – as they build blocks, arrange farm animals in their farm, vroom a small truck along an adventurous route under and over different pieces of furniture, and so on. And they practise what to say as they plan their play with peers or siblings, giving out stage directions as they assign roles, and specifying action sequences, as in:

John's older sister (4;0): I know, you can be the daddy and I can be the mummy. Yes?

John (2;0): *yes.*

(continued)

(continued)

J's older sister:	Right, we've got a baby haven't we?
John:	*yeah.*
J's older sister (addressing him by Father's real name):	Henry.
John:	*yeah*?
J's older sister:	Have you got any babies?
John (inaudible, then to adult observer):	*I a daddy.*

Part of children's practice requires the retrieval of words for the utterance being planned, the subsequent articulation of the utterance, and the use of appropriate timing in taking a turn, that is, coming in on time, as they participate in conversation. In planning an utterance ahead of time, children move from an idea of what to say, retrieve the relevant words, put them into an appropriate syntactic construction, and then utter them. None of this is easy, as shown by the long pauses, even between single-word utterances, from 1-year-olds, and the often-visible effort in young children as they try to label something or explain what they want. They have to practise in order to acquire the requisite fluency in production.

Taking turns

Coming in at the right place in conversation is another skill children take time to acquire. To do this, they need both fast retrieval of words as they listen to the other person speaking, and fluency in production for when they produce their own follow-up turn. In the first year, infants interact with adults by smiling, tracking gaze, watching hand motions, and, as they get older, vocalizing then babbling. But they often overlap with adult speech, and only start to establish a clear turn-taking pattern of one-speaker-at-a-time with exchange games like peek-a-boo or passing objects to and fro. As they begin to produce their first words, they often take a long time to get started on each turn. With just one adult interlocutor, they can rely on the adult to wait for them to speak. But older brothers and sisters won't wait, so 2-year-olds tend to lose out in exchanges with a parent and older sibling. And when they manage to take a turn, they come in too late, as much as two seconds too late. (A one-second pause in a conversation is long.) The place where their contribution would have been relevant has already been passed. As a result, what they say may seem irrelevant at the actual moment when it is produced.

In answering questions, children take time to come up with answers, so *yes/no* questions tend to be easier to answer, and faster, than early *Wh* questions. A few *Wh* questions can also be answered with a gesture – in *Where* and *Which* questions, for example. When asked *where* something is, 1-year-olds can simply point provided they have understood what the adult is asking about (e.g. 'Where's your bib?'); and when asked *which* thing they want (e.g. an apple or a plum), again, provided they understand the words for the entities being labelled, they can simply point at their choice. Early reliance on pointing gestures for answers shows that young children may have an answer available well before they can retrieve and say the relevant word(s).

What young children seem to realize rather early is that they need to respond, to take a turn, as soon as possible after the other speaker stops talking. And by age 2, some children have already adopted a strategy of initiating a turn with *Mmm* or *Uh* to signal they are about to talk but have not quite finished retrieving the necessary words. In short, production of words and utterances is intricately tied to the process of planning what to say.

Summary

Children can discriminate differences between sounds very early, and after a few months begin to recognize recurring sequences of sounds. Soon after this, they begin to attend to the sounds in the ambient language. Only after they can recognize and attach some meaning to such sequences do they begin to accumulate words in memory. Their representations for words are built on adult productions: children need to use these in order to recognize words from other speakers. They rely on the same representations of adult words as target forms when they try to produce specific words themselves.

Early word production is difficult, and early child forms are often not easily recognized. Children have to practise saying words, adjusting the word forms when they can so they become a better match to the adult target being aimed for. Children also need practice in retrieving the relevant words, in answering a question, for example, so that they come in on time in conversation. Attention to the timing in retrieval and in production more generally leads to greater fluency in language use.

Chapter 3

Mapping meanings to words

Forms without meanings can't be used effectively for communication. Children realize they have to identify the meaning (or part of the meaning) that a form conveys whenever they encounter an unfamiliar word. They have to solve what has been called the mapping problem. What does it take to map forms and meanings? Children need to identify the category-instance picked out by a referring expression like *the dog*, *the little train*, *the baby*, or *the flower*. That is, they need to learn what a particular word *refers* to, so they can identify the referent of any referring expression that contains that word. This initial identification of a referent may be a guess, be incomplete, or even be wrong, but children can adjust their preliminary assignment of meaning in light of adult usage. Adult feedback can refine initial guesses, and so enable children to arrive at a more satisfactory mapping. Together, adult uses and adult feedback allow children to update their mapping of forms and meanings.

(a) *Adam* (2;4.15): *wat dat?*
    Mother: What is that?
    Adam: *I don't know. giraffe. bunny-rabbit.*
    Mother: That's a kangaroo.
    Adam: **kangaroo**.

(continued)

(continued)

(b) *D* (2;8.14, with a toothbrush in his hand): *an' I going to tease.*

    Mother (puzzled):   Oh. Oh, you mean you're going to pretend to do your teeth?

    D: *yes.* (then, as father came by a minute later)

    Father: Are you going to do your teeth?

    D: *no, I was **pretending**.*

Getting the reference of a word right is one aspect of the acquisition of meaning. Children draw on both conceptual and social sources as they assign tentative meanings to new words. On the conceptual side, they build on categories already established in their first year. These include a variety of object-types, action-types, and relations that link objects to each other (a plate on a table, a ball next to a flowerpot), or link objects to actions (drinking from a cup, sitting on a chair). On the social side, they also make use of information inherent in adult-child interactions where adults talk about the immediate surroundings, the here-and-now. Children's existing knowledge of certain categories, along with the words offered by adults as they talk with their children, provides major input to the kind of mapping needed. To establish a preliminary mapping of a word-form and a meaning, children need to track the words adults use for objects and events on specific occasions.

Notice that referring expressions don't bear a one-to-one relation to their referents: speakers can use a variety of referring expressions to pick out the *same* entity on different occasions: *the dog, the spaniel, the guard, the barker, the dribbler,* or *that animal,* say, can all be used to refer to a specific dog. Similarly, a speaker can refer to a brick as *the brick, the book-end, the doorstop,* or *the step,* depending on the function assigned to the brick in each setting. The referring expression chosen by the speaker on each occasion presents the referent from a specific perspective to the person, the child, being addressed.

The other face of word meaning is the *sense* of a word – how it is connected to other words in the same semantic domain. Semantic domains are also often referred to as conceptual domains, and indeed typically represent conceptual domains. Take the word *horse*: it is related to the word *mammal* by inclusion: *a horse is a kind of mammal*. At the same time, *horse* is a cover term (a superordinate) for *stallion* and *mare* (adult male and female horses respectively), to the words *colt* and *filly* (immature males and females respectively), and to *foal* for a baby horse. As children build up their vocabularies, they learn how words are related to each other in meaning (their sense) and how they can be used to refer (their reference). And as they add more detail to the meaning of a word, they begin to group related words, words that share certain aspects of their meanings, into semantic domains.

Consider the domain of birds. Young children typically start with just a few terms for birds, *duck* (on the water), *chicken* (on the ground), and *bird* (flying in the air), say. They gradually add more terms and discover that the term *bird* is superordinate to *duck* and *chicken* and *owl*, that several kinds of birds swim (*duck, goose, swan*), that most birds fly (*swallow, owl, pigeon, woodpecker*), and that there are further subdivisions of birds – those active in the day versus at night; sea birds; water birds; song birds; predators, and so on. But organizing, and reorganizing, each sub-domain here depends on children's acquisition of the relevant words for the categories and subcategories in question.

Children follow the same course with respect to words for actions and relations within events. They must identify the forms for talking about particular actions and relations. For example, they need to identify actions that count as 'throwing', 'running', 'eating', 'drinking', 'feeding', 'breaking', and 'opening', and map these to the adult words. They also need to identify relations that would count as 'being in' or 'putting in', 'being on', 'going into' versus 'going out of', 'going up' versus 'going down', 'between', 'along', 'under', and 'beside'. Their mappings here depend on knowledge of the relation and of the relevant properties of the figure (the moveable or moving object) and its relation to the ground or landmark where it is placed or is moving. In this mapping, children must attend to how each word is used to refer to the pertinent category, and how it is related to neighbours in that semantic domain.

Adults are a major source of information for children about words and how words are related to each other in meaning. Common relations that link word meanings include how things are related in terms of class-membership or inclusion (*a raccoon is a kind of animal*), part-to-whole (*those are the rabbit's ears*), function (*the sieve is for straining rice*), ontogenesis (*a foal is a baby horse*), and any other kind of information that links the **senses** of words. Children must also identify the **reference** of any referring expressions that adults make use of in talking with them. These are expressions that pick out specific objects, actions, and relations in context, from a particular perspective. Sense and reference together constitute the two 'faces' of meanings that children have to work out.

Fast mapping

The first step in linking a form and meaning is fast mapping, which depends on joint attention, physical co-presence, and conversational co-presence (see further Chapter 4). Children assign a preliminary meaning in context upon hearing a new word, and then use that word accordingly, until they notice that their usage doesn't match the adult's, or until they get more information about that word meaning. Evidence for fast, and incomplete, mapping is available from children's early over-extensions of many words, when they stretch a word to refer to things *not* covered in adult usage. They over-extend between 40 per cent and 60 per cent of their early words, generally when their production vocabulary is still quite small at 100–200 words. Some typical examples based on shape, movement, and size are shown below. Young children also base some over-extensions on texture, taste, and sound. But most over-extensions depend on similarities of shape.

The over-extensions recorded by diarists are remarkably similar across languages: children take into account the first referent and start from that in extending and, often, over-extending the word. These over-extensions are most prevalent between age 1;0 and 2;6. Each one lasts for anything from a few days to several months. They appear to depend on communicative need at a time when children have only a very small vocabulary. But as children add further information about word-meanings to their initial fast mapping, and as they add more words relevant to a particular domain, they narrow down their over-extensions to achieve a closer match to the conventional adult meaning and adult usage.

Lexical item	First referent	Extensions/over-extensions in order of occurrence
mooi	moon	cakes; round marks on window; writing on window/in books; round shapes in books; tooling on book covers; round postmarks; letter O
buti	ball	toy; radish; stone spheres at park entrance
ticktock	watch	clocks; all clocks and watches; gas meter; fire hose on spool; bath-scale with round dial
kutija	box	matchbox; drawer; bedside table
cotty-bars	bars of cot	large toy abacus; toast-rack; building with columns
titi	animals	pictures of animals; things that move
bird	sparrows	cows; dogs; cats; any animal moving
tutu	train	engine; moving train; journey
fly	fly	specks of dirt; dust; small insects; own toes; bread-crumbs; toad
pin	pin	crumb; caterpillars
koko	cock crowing	tunes on violin; tunes on piano; tunes on accordion; tunes on phonograph; all music; merry-go-round

Adding more information about the meaning of a new word may arise quite naturally after an adult offer of a new word, as in the following exchange:

Child (1;8.12, looking at picture of owls in new book): *duck. duck.*
Mother: Yeah, those are birds. <looks at picture>
They're called owls. <points at picture>
Owls, that's their name. Owls. <looks at child>
Child: **birds**.
Mother: And you know what the owl says?
<points at the picture again> The owl goes 'hoo'. 'hoo'.

(continued)

(continued)

Child:	**owl**.
Mother:	That's what the owl says.
Child:	**hoo**. <smiles>
Mother:	that's right.

Notice that the child ratifies each piece of information offered – that the picture is of birds, that the birds are owls, and that they say 'hoo'. She does this by repeating the words *birds*, *owl*, and *hoo* in successive turns. Effectively, by supplying added information beyond the label *owl*, the adult here places this new category of birds into the appropriate domain (alongside ducks) and provides the child with distinctive information about them (the sound they make). Adults often supply information about class membership or inclusion along with new words. They also add information about properties and parts of the referent, functions (if there is one), and motion, along with other details such as habitat, food, and young.

Eliciting and retaining new words

Children recognize, fairly early on, that there are conventional words for things, and, from 1;6 onwards, ask 'What's that?' with increasing frequency. These questions appear designed to elicit relevant words from the more expert adult speakers. But children's retention of these new words appears weak. When tested on their comprehension and production of words they have been exposed to in experimental settings, children under 2;6 show little retention just twenty-four hours later. As they get older, they get faster at uptake, often try to say new words as soon as they hear them, and retain more of the words they have been exposed to. In a more natural setting for learning new words – from storybooks – they tend to retain more new words when they are read one story several times, compared to different stories containing the same number of target words. The contexts for new words, with repeated exposures, then, appear to help children fix an initial mapping of their meanings.

What is important here are the opportunities children have to pick up new words. They encounter many unfamiliar words just in conversation. Many of these words are ones where children have to make inferences in context about meaning. Their inferences may be supported by subsequent adult uses, and by adult acceptance of the children's uses. On other occasions, children may misuse a new word they have heard, and then get explicit feedback from adults. This feedback typically offers further examples of adult usage. On other occasions still, children take up explicit offers of new words, along with added information about the referent object, action, or relation. These explicit offers are often accompanied by additional information, as in the *owl*-exchange just considered. These patterns of uptake, usage, and feedback are readily observed in spontaneous conversation between adult and child.

Researchers have also used experimental tasks to explore early word learning. The general concern has been with assignment of some meaning (with fast mapping) to a nonsense word, in contexts where there is one unfamiliar referent and one familiar one. Children infer that the new word they hear must go with, refer to, the unfamiliar object. (Otherwise, the speaker would have used the familiar word already known to the child.) These studies established that children do fast mapping: they assign some meaning to newly encountered words right away. But, depending on their age and the number of exposures, they may not remember a new word for long. Researchers have also shown that the context of exposure for a new word influences children's assignment of the word to pick out an object category or an action category. However, these experimental studies have yet to explore the roles of feedback and further adult usage in children's uptake of new words. Lastly, another ingredient central to children's word-learning is the practice they get in using new words. But this also requires further exposure in a range of contexts. The more practice children have, the more feedback they get, and hence more opportunities to add to, refine, or change the meaning first assigned to a new word.

Early vocabularies

Where do children get their first words? From the ambient language that surrounds their own activities. Adults, remember, talk with their children about the here-and-now, about what they are doing and playing with at that moment, in that place. Which words do children typically produce early on, in their first 100 or so? And do all young children talk first about similar things and so produce similar words, regardless of language, in their first year of talking? There are strong similarities in the kinds of words produced first across children and languages. But as children get older, there is more divergence in the range of things children have words for, depending on social class and the language being acquired.

Children talk about the people around them, about household objects, toys, food and drink, clothing, animals, vehicles, and a few body-part terms between 1;0 and 1;6. They also talk about certain child-oriented activities and events, everyday routines, and about sounds and motion. Common words produced in each of these categories are shown in the box below.

People: daddy, mommy (1;0), baby (1;3), grandma, grandpa (1;6)
Food/drink: banana, juice, cookie (1;4), cracker, apple, cheese (1;5)
Body parts: eye, nose (1;4), ear (1;5)
Clothing: shoe (1;4), sock, hat (1;6)
Animals: dog (1;2), kitty, bird, duck (1;4), cat, fish (1;6)
Vehicles: car (1;4), truck (1;6)
Toys: ball (1;3), book, balloon (1;4), boat (1;6)
Household objects: bottle (1;4), keys (1;5)
Routines: bye (1;1), hi (1;2), no (1;3), night-night (1;4),
    bath, peek-a-boo (1;5), thank you (1;6)
Activities (sound effects, motion, state): uh-oh (1;2), woof, moo,
    ouch, baa-baa, yum-yum (1;4), vroom, up, down (1;5)

The ages here reflect the median age at which children produce each word listed (i.e. half the children in a large normed sample produced it earlier, half later than the age given).

By age 2, children produce anywhere between 50 and over 500 word types (this is the normal range in production vocabulary at this age), and they use their words strategically to pick out particular roles in events, as when they name the person entering the room (*dada*), refer to the state of sitting or stepping down with *down*, or indicate that they want to go outside with *step!* (from 'mind the step'). During their first year of talking, children add steadily to their repertoires, adding words gleaned from everyday interactions and, perhaps especially, from book-reading sessions with parents.

Building up lexical domains

Children start out slowly and, as we saw in Chapter 2, their early word productions are often unrecognizable and their meanings sometimes mis-mapped. It takes time to add new words in production, and also time for them to produce a recognizable version of each word. Most of the early words children produce in English tend to be words for objects, with only a few words for actions. The balance between words for objects versus actions differs across languages. It depends partly on whether expressions like *the boy* can be omitted on the speaker's second mention in a language (such omissions are called argument ellipsis). For example, in languages like Japanese or Korean, with more ellipsis, parents use many verbs, often more verbs than nouns. As a result, children acquiring those languages tend to have more words for actions (verbs) at a young age than children acquiring English.

As children add more words in production, they build up sub-vocabularies for different domains. They accumulate words for animals, adding to early terms like *dog* and *kitty* with terms for farm animals and animals found in zoos, and more specialized terms still as they learn about the habitats for animals like sea otters, chipmunks, and vervet monkeys. Along with these new animal terms, they will also add verbs for the motions and activities of each animal – the way it moves (*walk*, *trot*, *canter*, *gallop*, for example), the noise it makes (*neigh*, *whinny*), its habitat (*stable*, *paddock*, *field*, *hills*), and what it eats (*grass*, *oats*, *hay*). Such domains take time to build up, and many remain incomplete, even for adults.

They also add to their terms for vehicles (e.g. *car*, *boat*, *plane*, *bicycle*, *sled*, *cart*, *scooter*) and for subtypes of cars, say. They add words for all the main body parts, usually getting upper-body terms before lower-body ones; they add words for different items of clothing, for different foods and utensils in use at mealtimes. And they add words for different toys. They also add words for activities associated with different objects such as clothes, pop-beads, and blocks: *put on* and *take off, put in* or *on, open, shut*; and words for their own activities: *walk, run, sit, play, paddle, swim, dig*. In linking objects and actions, roles and events, they gradually map more of the conceptual space around them into language. In doing this, children add words for additional (sub)domains in their vocabulary, then elaborate each domain and set up new domains as they learn and add new words.

Space, motion, goal, and source

When children map terms for motion in space, they must attend to properties of the figure (the entity that is moving or being placed somewhere) and of the ground. One-year-olds show an early preference for containers to be oriented with the opening facing up (a box, a jam jar, a bowl) and for placing small objects inside such containers. That is, given a choice of placing something in or beside a container, they always place it in. They display other early preferences as well: objects belong on top of surfaces (not underneath or beside). And objects should be juxtaposed-in-contact with any larger reference point or ground, rather than be placed a short distance away from it. That is, proximity-with-contact is preferred over open spaces left between figure and ground.

Conceptual organizing principles like these provide one basis for a first mapping of spatial terms like *in* and *on* in English, for both static and dynamic relations, where the child places or moves one object in relation to another. However, mapping such relations to words differs across languages. In Korean, the verbs for placement 'in' also take into account whether the fit between figure and ground is tight (e.g. a cassette in its plastic case), or loose (e.g. an apple in a bowl). This attention to tight versus loose fit determines which verb the speaker uses on each occasion. And by age 2, Korean-speaking children consistently distinguish the two.

Notice too that while 'in' in English covers both tight and loose fit in both static and dynamic spatial relations, 'in' can also be extended to non-spatial domains like time (*in a moment*), state (*in a huff*), and pitch (*in C-major*). Much the same applies to 'on', which can be extended to non-supporting surfaces (*on the wall, on the ceiling*) and to time (*on Friday*). Such patterns of extension are sometimes language-specific, so children may follow slightly different paths in the acquisition of spatial terms in different languages.

Talk about motion in space presents another area of the lexicon where languages differ in their mapping. Consider the English verbs *stroll* and *run*: *stroll* conveys the meaning of motion with a leisurely, slow manner, while *run* conveys rapid motion in space. Some languages, like English, consistently combine information about manner and motion in verbs of motion: consider *wander, meander, stroll, jog, run*, and *race*. Information about the direction of motion is then added with a prepositional phrase: *wander <u>towards the river</u>, jog <u>round the pond</u>, run <u>up the hill</u>*. Other languages instead combine information about motion and direction in the verb, and add manner separately, as in Spanish *subir* 'go + up', *bajar* 'go + down', or *entrar* 'go + in'. (English has a few verbs like this too.) Information about manner can be added in Spanish with a verbal participle (*corriendo* 'running', *flotando* 'floating'), or be inferred from information given about the terrain where the motion occurs (across a ploughed field versus down a cliff path, for example). Children have to figure out first whether the verbs of motion they hear combine motion and manner, or motion and direction. They are generally helped by the presence of prepositional phrases that identify the goal of the motion, for example, *He ran <u>into the house</u>*. In Spanish, instead one says, *Corrió a casa y entró* 'he ran to the house and went in'. That is, one runs up to a goal and then crosses into it. The same event is mapped differently onto the verbs in the two languages. Children have to identify the relevant patterns for the mapping in the language they are acquiring, and assign the appropriate meanings to their verbs of motion.

Speech act meanings

Children rely on gestures, especially pointing and reaching, to convey their interest in an object or event (by pointing at it), or their desire for something (by reaching towards it). These proto-speech acts emerge at around 10 months. Pointing is soon supplemented with words: *that*, *there*, or a label for the object in question, *kitty*. And reaching may be marked with added intensity in the form of whining, later replaced by words like *want*, *want-it*, or *gimme*. Pointing, then, appears to be a precursor to assertions, while reaching is a precursor to requests.

Only later do children understand and add further speech acts such as promising or warning. To manage this, they need to make the inferences appropriate to the speaker's intention on each occasion. They must also learn the social conventions for such acts as greeting or saying farewell, requesting politely (*please* . . .), and thanking, along with the social formulas for carrying out these acts. Finally, they also need to learn performative speech acts, where the act is achieved in the process of issuing the utterance, as in: *I name this child Sophie*. And she is thereby named. Construing the speaker's intention, then, involves identifying the speech act being used for each utterance. This in turn allows children to map an utterance as a request, a promise, or an assertion, depending on the speaker, the occasion, and the context (see further Chapter 7).

Construction meanings

Constructions also have meanings and so add a further dimension to the words they contain, by presenting them in particular combinations and frames. The verb *walk*, for example, can appear in an intransitive construction with a subject and verb (*He is walking*) or in a transitive construction, with a subject-verb-object order (*He walks the dog*). Or take the terms *cat*, *dog*, and *chase*. If we place them in a transitive construction in English, with subject-verb-object order, we could get *The dog chased the cat*. The construction identifies the roles, with the referent of the first noun phrase (the subject) identifying the agent of the action described by the verb. This agent (*the dog*) acts on the object (the referent of the second noun phrase, *the cat*). Other constructions add different meanings. The intransitive construction identifies the agent or actor, the only role involved with the action, as in *The boy ran (along the path)*. The added phrase, *along the path*, provides information about the location of the action. This information can be added to transitive constructions too. Causative constructions assign a meaning we could summarize as [Agent – CAUSE-CHANGE-OF-STATE – Object-affected], as in *Tommy broke the branch.* Here, the causing event is one of breaking, with Tommy as the agent and the branch as the object-affected. Different constructions contribute added meaning to the nouns and verbs they contain (see further Chapters 5 and 6.)

Reference and referential expressions

As children try to follow what someone is talking about, they need to identify the referents of any expressions the speaker produces: *the fish, that stone, some apple sauce.* Where these referential expressions contain familiar words, children can follow more easily what the speaker intends to talk about. But they also need to know how demonstratives (*this, that*) and pronouns (*he, you, they*) work, since these, too, refer, and often mark successive references by the speaker.

The mapping that children infer depends from the start on their grasp of word meanings. They need to identify the referent being mentioned, and track further references to that entity throughout a communicative exchange. Young children get some practice with this when adults offer alternative versions of what they are trying to convey, e.g. *Pick up <u>the blocks</u>, Put <u>the blocks</u> into the box, Put <u>the red blocks</u> away*, and so on. And when they listen to stories, they can track pictures of the same object from page to page as they hear the adult refer to it: *Peter Rabbit, the little rabbit, he* . . . Keeping track of what the speaker is talking about depends on children's having identified at least part of the conventional meaning of a word, and hence its possible reference. On top of that, they may need to infer the relation between the adult's utterance and the current situation. These inferences in turn depend on the adult and child jointly attending to the same thing, to entities and activities that are physically present, and to any familiar words in the ongoing conversation. Consider a scenario where the adult starts with 'It's cold in here'. Children as young as 2 readily make the inference that the adult would like it to be warmer, and look for a way to achieve this, for instance, by closing an open door or window.

Terms with shifting reference	
(a) *I – you*	Speaker
(b) *here – there*	Speaker & Place
(c) *this – that*	Speaker & Place & Object
(d) *come – go*	Speaker & Place & Object & Motion
(e) *bring – take*	Speaker & Place & Object & Motion & Cause

Among early referential expressions are pronouns like *I* and *you*, along with the third-person forms *he*, *she*, *it*, and *they*. Pronouns are deictic: they 'point' at the person referred to. Third-person forms, for example, pick out individual referents in context. But some of them are special: *I* is always the current speaker, *you* the current addressee(s). *I* and *you* are also so-called shifters: the referent of *I* shifts every time there is a change of speaker just as the referent of *you* also changes in any two-person exchange. But early on, children don't always grasp the shifting nature of these pronouns and may use *I* for the adult and *you* for the child instead, with utterances like *Pick you up* (= pick me up) or *You want milk* (= I want milk). This is more likely in first-born than in second-born children, who get direct evidence from their older siblings that *I* and *you* have shifting reference.

Other deictic terms that shift in the same way as *I* and *you* include the locative terms *here* and *there*, the demonstratives *this* and *that* (also *these* and *those*), and also, in English, the verbs *come* and *go*, *bring* and *take*. In general, children acquire the pronoun pair *I* and *you* first, the least complex of these deictic shifters, at around age 2 to 2;6, and then go on master more complex terms in this domain. Each pair of terms is tied to a deictic centre, namely the speaker, and whether the reference is to the speaker, to the place where the speaker is versus elsewhere (compare *here in the house*, *here in California*, *here in America*, *here in the Western world*), depending on the comparison being invoked. The same holds for use of *this* versus *that*, and their plural forms, and for the verbs *come* versus *go*, and their causative counterparts *bring* and *take* or *send*.

Summary

Children acquire meanings gradually. They take up words in context and assign them a preliminary meaning. This first step is called fast mapping. But meaning assigned this way corresponds only roughly to the conventional adult meaning. So children have to adjust these first meanings in light of further uses from adults and of feedback from adults about their own uses. As they learn more words, children organize them into semantic domains: they elaborate and reorganize each domain as they add still more words. The words in a semantic domain are linked by various semantic relations that involve inclusion, parts, properties, function, characteristic motion, and so on. These relations link the meanings of terms within a domain, as well as across neighbouring domains. These relations depend on the senses of words. But this is just one face of word meaning – the other face is reference: words used in referring expressions to pick out specific referents on particular occasions.

Children also take into account what speakers intend to talk about when they produce particular referring expressions in particular constructions. To do this, children need to do two things: they must attend to the current common ground and to what is in joint attention for the adult and child on each occasion. And they must also take into account the meanings of constructions as well as of the nouns and verbs appearing in each construction used. We return to this in Chapters 7 and 8.

Chapter 4

Using language

We turn next to children's pragmatic skills and when they invoke these in the course of acquiring a first language. Pragmatic skills are those skills involved in language use: keeping track of common ground; designing utterances to express the speaker's intention in such a way that the current addressee will arrive readily at the intended interpretation; making the appropriate inferences in context given what the speaker is saying, and so on. Indeed, children (like adults) rely on making inferences in context about what is going on as they participate in all kinds of communicative exchanges. These inferences are called pragmatic inferences, where 'pragmatic' generally has to do with usage in context, and context here includes both the current physical context and any common ground shared with the speaker. For example, when you hear a speaker say 'the birch tree', you could infer that the speaker is talking about a tree that has already been mentioned and is therefore in common ground for the speaker and addressee. If instead, you hear 'a birch tree', you would then look around for a possible referent for that expression: the referent is not yet in common ground. We also rely on such inferences to link clauses. If you hear 'The picnic basket is in the car. The lemonade is still cold', you infer that the lemonade was in or was part of the picnic supplies. That is, we make pragmatic inferences all the time in relating speakers' utterances to objects, activities, and relations in the world. And our inferences are driven in large part by what we infer about the speaker's intention on that occasion, the goal that that speaker has in talking.

Children start communicating what they are interested in from around 10 or 12 months on. They point at objects and events that catch their attention; they reach for objects that they want. When they point, adults typically name the objects and events being attended to: 'That's a pussy cat', 'Oh look at the ducks', 'That boy is climbing a tree'. And when children this age reach for something, they persist in reaching (and whining) or pointing insistently until the adult identifies what it is they want: at mealtimes for example, a particular kind of fruit, a specific food – at which point the children may relax, stop reaching, and wait for the adult to give it to them.

(a) *A* (1;0.28, looks and reaches towards food on table)
Mother (looks at food):   What do you want? <looks at baby>
A <continues to reach>
Mother (looks at A, offers food): This?
A (looks at Mother, accepts food)

(b) B (1;0.21, looks above and behind Mother, leans and points in direction of look)
Mother (looks at B, offers food): Hmm?
B (looks at food, bounces in high chair, pushes food away, then looks behind Mother)
Mother (looks at B, offers food): Want some?
B (withdraws from offer)
Mother (looks at B):   No?
B (shakes head 'no' and bounces in high chair)
Mother (withdraws offer of food)
B (looks at food)
Mother (looks at B, offers food)
B (accepts food and vocalizes, eats)

They also 'ask' adults to open boxes or jars by holding them up, again persisting until the adult helps them. Such reliance on gesture and gaze by 12-month-olds suggests that they are eager to communicate with their caregivers. This impulse appears to be one driver in the process of acquisition.

Children's early reliance on pointing and reaching gestures can be viewed as antecedents to the speech acts of asserting (*I'm looking at that*) and requesting (*I want that*). Gestural proto-speech acts are widely used by young children who are just getting to the stage where they can produce a few single-word utterances. Children also make use of gestures to answer some adult questions: 'Where are your shoes?' – [Child points]. Adults use gestures in part to manage what children are doing, in part to attract and maintain their attention on what the adult is talking about. In short, children start out with the means they have available, primarily gestures and gaze, before they add words for what they are trying to communicate.

Pragmatic principles

Pragmatic principles are concerned with how language use is made effective. They capture the practices of speakers and addressees as they focus on communicating effectively. An overarching pragmatic principle of language use, observed by adults, is the **Cooperative Principle**. Speakers cooperate in talking with each other. They take account of what each person already knows, and what they can each reasonably infer from information offered by the speaker. Children observe this kind of cooperation from early on, but they take several years to grasp what being fully cooperative entails. For example, to be cooperative in conversation means they should (a) be truthful, (b) be relevant, (c) be clear, and (d) provide as much information as is required. Children, though, take time to learn what counts as being fully cooperative in an exchange, for instance in assessing how much information to provide when they answer a question. The Cooperative Principle can only work, of course, if speakers are agreed on how to communicate – appropriately identifying the best words and constructions to use to convey specific meanings on particular occasions.

Speakers also observe two additional principles that guide language use: **conventionality** and **contrast**. Conventionality captures the fact that, for certain meanings, speakers assume that there is a conventional form in the language community that should be used. Speakers then expect each other to use available conventional forms for conveying their intended meanings. If they don't use the expected form on a particular occasion but instead coin a new word, say, then addressees infer that the speaker must mean something else – namely, whatever is captured in context by the speaker's coinage on that occasion. Entry into any linguistic community depends on acquisition of the conventional form-meaning pairings in the language. These are what adults transmit to children as they talk with them.

Conventionality goes hand in hand with another pragmatic principle, contrast. This captures the fact that speakers assume that any difference in form signals a difference in meaning – there are no *true* synonyms in language. In other words, two distinct forms can't have exactly the same meaning. Notice the asymmetry here: a single form can have several distinct meanings. This is because speakers readily extend word meanings, stretching them to cover similar or related instances. The term *head* designates the body part, but it has been extended in English to the notion of the main person responsible: 'head of the school', 'headmistress', 'head of government/state'; and has been extended still further in such uses as 'head of the valley' and 'head of the bed'.

Children grasp and make use of both conventionality and contrast very early in acquisition. When they hear terms like *big* and *bag*, they assume they must have different meanings, just as *ball* and *bell* do, or *ball*, *call*, *hall*, and *tall*. Notice that observing contrast gives children a boost in mapping forms and meanings: different forms must have different meanings, so children have no need to check whether the meaning of a new word coincides with that of any word they already know. If the form is unfamiliar, the word must have a meaning that differs from the meanings of words already known. Reliance on conventionality and contrast is also basic for adult usage.

Common ground

One factor in being cooperative in conversation is attending to what the other person does (and doesn't) know. This is critical for how speakers design their utterances. One reason for this is that the course of a conversation depends on **common ground**, what the participants all know in common and know that they each know. In establishing common ground, speakers (here, adult and child) need to attend to what their addressees both do and don't know already, and then keep track of information being added to common ground in the course of an exchange.

What counts as common ground? Common ground includes information known to both speaker and addressee. This information can be cultural: 'we grew up in the same country', 'we speak the same language', 'we work in the same field'. It can also involve more specific information: 'we both like birdwatching', 'we both know how to play tennis', or 'we all like aubergines'. While establishing such cultural common ground is often the topic of a first conversation with someone new, speakers also accumulate common ground in the course of each conversation as they each contribute new information. When this new information is taken up and acknowledged by the other, it is thereby placed in the current common ground.

How do speakers manage this? In particular, how do adults manage this as they talk with young children? Speakers depend on joint attention, on physical co-presence, and on conversational co-presence. With adults, joint attention is readily attained, but with children under 2 or 3, adults generally either follow in to whatever the child is attending to at that moment, or else attract and then hold on to the child's attention, typically with both gestures and words. The focus of this joint attention is typically an object or event that is physically present at that moment. The adult speaker generally relies on conversational co-presence as well, through the use of familiar words alongside any that are new to the child.

But children's attention at age 12 to 18 months is also limited by their field of view. When an 18-month-old holds a toy truck with both hands and looks at it, that child's field of vision is largely filled by the truck alone. So what children this age attend to is often very limited. This in turn makes adult labels, offered at just the right moment, all the more easy to map onto the right referents. That is, provided adults time their offers of words to just those moments when young children are attending directly to what they are holding and looking at, children should find it relatively easy to map word forms and preliminary meanings.

Such mapping is facilitated because reliance on conventionality, contrast, and the Cooperative Principle in conversation depends on joint attention, physical co-presence, and conversational co-presence. With joint attention, adult and child can be sure they are attending to the same entity or the same event; with physical co-presence, adult and child can be sure that what they are attending to in the current setting is what the speaker is currently concerned with. Finally, conversational co-presence allows the child to make use of any familiar words alongside any new ones, as the adult speaker talks about what is in the locus of their joint attention. (We discuss common ground further in Chapter 7.)

Scaffolding and collaboration

In talking to young children, adults generally depend on common ground they have already established with the child: events known to them both, and readily evoked by the adult's provision of information about the relevant setting, or by the child's allusion to some salient detail of an event. The adult typically scaffolds or sets up framing so the young child can supply just single words where needed when the adult pauses on a rising intonation contour. Such scaffolding sets young children up as conversational partners at a stage when they are not yet competent turn-takers.

Common ground plays a critical role in all such scaffolding because, without common ground, the adult cannot offer an appropriate setting where the child can simply contribute the relevant words at the right point in time. Consider the two exchanges that follow. In the first, the adult is a stranger to the child and knows nothing about the history of the child's Band-Aid; in the second, the mother and child share common ground – both know the history of the Band-Aid, so the mother can offer the appropriate scaffolding:

Meredith (1;6), talking to an unfamiliar adult
Meredith: *Band-Aid.*
Adult: Where's your Band-Aid?
Meredith: *Band-Aid.*
Adult: Do you have a Band-Aid?
Meredith: *Band-Aid.*
Adult: Did you fall down and hurt yourself?

And then, a few minutes later, when her mother comes into the room:

Meredith (1;6), talking to her mother about the same event
Meredith: *Band-Aid.*
Mother: Who gave you the Band-Aid?
Meredith: *nurse.*
Mother: Where did she put it?
Meredith: *arm.*

Notice that in both cases, Meredith initiated the exchange: she wanted to talk about her Band-Aid, but was unable to follow the right steps without scaffolding, scaffolding that depended critically on the mother's knowledge about the event. The turns in such exchanges are a collaborative affair between adult and child. The adult speaker provides the general framework and the given information in each utterance, and the child, on cue, provides the critical noun or verb that picks out some new information.

Turns and their content

Early patterns of interaction involve extensive infant attention to the adult, with gaze and vocalization. And infant vocalizations often overlap with any adult speech. It takes time to learn to take turns: children may be aged 9 or 10 months before they become proficient at taking turns in exchange games and peek-a-boo. Yet adults present young infants with a framework for turn-taking, starting as young as 3 months. It is at that stage that an adult will say something, then wait until the infant emits an action – a smile, a burp, a foot-kick – that could be construed as a 'turn', after which the adult says something more. Adults may impose these early turns where they are willing to wait longer than normal for the child's contribution. Indeed, timing here tends to depart quite widely from actual adult-like turn-taking in conversation. This is because it is dictated by how soon after an adult utterance ends the infant actually does something that can be counted as a turn (see also Chapter 2).

What is the content of infant and young-child turns? While adults use words and gestures, infants rely extensively on gestures, sometimes on actions, and then, as they get older, they make more and more use of single words, then word-combinations, and then longer and longer utterances. Adults generally seem to take anything occurring within three seconds of the end of an adult utterance as being the next turn in an exchange. In adult–adult exchanges in English, though, adults answer *yes/no* questions within 300 milliseconds, with a median time of less than 100 milliseconds. In studies of how fast young children can answer questions, researchers have found that they are considerably slower than adults. Once they have an answer to give, they may use gestures in response to a *Where* or *Which* question, and these gestures are produced faster in their answers than words are. And in their verbal answers, they produce words repeated from the adult question faster than 'new' words retrieved from memory. So planning an answer clearly depends on how hard it is to retrieve the relevant information and the relevant words, and then to produce the answer.

Lastly, once young children realize that they need to respond 'on time' to questions and comments within a conversation, they begin to make use of ways to hold the floor even when they are not actually ready to take their next turn. Like adults, they rely early on terms like *mm*, *well*, *uh*, and *um* in order to signal that they are ready to take their turn but haven't quite got the content of that turn ready to emit, as well as other delay markers that indicate they are not quite ready to talk at the start of their turn.

(a) Hesitation marker: ***um*, *uh***
(b) Repetition: ***but but but but but*** *we could sing some other songs* (3;1)
(c) Restart word: ***liz– lizards*** *nurse* (1;10)
(d) Fronting of word: ***wool*** *cut her wool* (1;11)
(e) Prolongation: ***uh–*** *just brown* (3;1)

Grounding successive utterances

Speakers ground each utterance as it occurs in an exchange. That is, once speakers begin an exchange, they may start from any existing common ground, or else begin by first establishing some preliminary common ground. They then add to that common ground with each successive utterance in the exchange as it goes on. Ideally, the information flow from one utterance to the next will reflect this in that each speaker will start an utterance with given or already-known information and then add to that something new. The next speaker will then acknowledge the new information from the prior turn, treating it now as given, and then add to that something more that is new. Each piece of information is thus added to the common ground the speakers are making use of within the current exchange.

New information can be acknowledged in several ways: with *uh-huh*, *yeah*, *yes*, and so on, or quite explicitly with a repeat of all or part of the new information from the preceding utterance. The repeat indicates clearly that that speaker has taken up the new information and, by repeating it, has added it to common ground. Like adults, young children acknowledge or repeat new information from a young age, as in Abe's follow-up utterance in the exchange here:

> *Abe* (2;5.10): *I want butter mine.*
> *Father:* OK give it here and I'll put butter on it.
> *Abe:* *I need butter **on it**.*

When young children don't acknowledge with an *uh-huh*, a *yeah*, or a repeat, they instead often continue on the same topic, adding further (new) information relevant to the prior speaker's utterance. Such continuations also show that they have understood the adult's earlier turns.

Early on, 1- and 2-year-olds may acknowledge new information from the other speaker, but add nothing new themselves. By 2;0 to 2;6, though, they are often able to ground new information from another speaker, *and* add new information themselves. Doing this, of course, also demands fluency in producing the relevant word choices and constructions. In shifting the status of some information from new to given, a speaker may simply repeat it, or, in the case of a lexical referring expression (*the dog*), switch to a pronoun (*it*). In talking about an action, the switch may be from a lexical verb (*open, break, eat*) to a general-purpose verb like *do* or *make*, or to an aspectual verb like *finish* that focusses on the end-point of an action. Young children, though, especially under age 6, tend to use pronouns for most referents that are visible (in a picture book, say), apparently taking for granted the addressee's ability to see those referents, as in this telling of a story about a little boy who gets a balloon that he then loses:

> *He's* (= boy) *walking along . . . and he* (= boy) *sees a balloon man . . . and he* (= man) *gives him a green one* (= balloon) *. . . and he* (= boy) *walks off home . . . and it* (= balloon) *flies away into the sky. so he* (= boy) *cries.*

Children take time to master pronouns for referring to something that has already been more fully identified with a lexical noun phrase, as in *The little boy... he... he...* In telling this story, for example, 4-year-olds can move from a noun phrase to a pronoun in references to the main character, but they often start out with a pronoun for that character from the start, as in the version of the story just given. The other characters are generally referred to with nouns only (e.g. *the balloon man*). This can be seen in another version of the same story – based on the same series of six pictures – of a little's boy's encounter with a balloon man, and his subsequent loss of the balloon he'd been given. (Successive references to the main character are underlined.)

---

a little boy is walking along. *he* sees a balloon seller.
he wants a green balloon. *he* gets one. *he* walks off in
the sunshine. *he* lets go of the balloon and then *he* starts crying.

Children also, of course, often point at the relevant character as they are talking, so these pronoun references are generally clear in context.

Inferences about intended meaning

Children make inferences not only from the context of a speaker's utterance, but also from the words used. Speakers choose their words to be as informative as needed on that occasion. They choose referring expressions and other terms that they judge will best convey their meaning. For example, a speaker might say 'Some of the cherries are ripe' as an invitation to pick cherries but to be selective about it. The same speaker might later on say, 'The cherries are ripe' or 'All the cherries are ripe' as a general invitation to pick the fruit. Children must learn which inferences to make as they consider just what the speaker intends on each occasion.

Contrast clearly plays a role here, and in some cases, children's (and adults') inferences depend on being able to access a particular contrast set. That is, they need to have in mind what the alternatives are. Take *some* versus *all*. If a speaker uses *some*, as in 'Some of the cherries are ripe', the general inference here is 'not all the cherries are ripe'. That is, choice of the quantifier *some* has as its alternative here *all* (or rather, *not all*). Another alternative may be *none*, for a scale that contains < *none* ~ *some* ~ *all* >. Children under 4 or 5 have difficulty dealing with such scales, and may fail to make the appropriate inferences. But when presented with explicit information about relevant alternatives, they do better, e.g. when asked 'Does the boy have just some apples, or *all* the fruit – bananas too – in his box?' (asked of a boy holding a box with some fruit in it), or, 'Are *all* the animals sleeping?' (when only two of three animals are asleep). When the alternatives are clear, children answer such questions in an adult-like fashion. This suggests that being able to come up with the relevant alternatives plays a role in making such inferences. It also suggests that it is further experience with language that allows children to identify such scales as < *a few* ~ *more* ~ *all* >, or < *none* ~ *some* ~ *all* >.

Identifying the relevant alternatives in context may be quite difficult. What are the alternatives to *the cat* when that is used as a referring expression? Do they include references to any other type of animal in the vicinity? Or what might the alternatives be to *the red car*? The colour term *red* picks out only one of many colours. Maybe generating a set of alternatives simply becomes more critical when one is dealing with how to map quantifying expressions like *some* and *all*.

Summary

Children's ability to understand and use language depends on some fundamental pragmatic principles: cooperation, conventionality, and contrast. They start observing these principles early on, but take several years to fully master how to use them most effectively in conversational exchanges. Effective use of these pragmatic principles depends on children's grasp of common ground – what they and their interlocutors know at each turn in an exchange and hence on joint attention. They need to track what happens at each step in a conversation so they can make relevant contributions in their own turns. Adults help here by scaffolding early conversational exchanges and waiting for the child's contribution. But as children acquire more language – and more fluency – they must learn how to contribute to multi-party conversations as well as to simpler dyadic ones. It is only by tracking what happens in each turn, the content of what each speaker contributes, that children can contribute themselves.

Chapter 5

Early constructions

Children start small because they have to. They use language in the simplest way possible because they know very little. But as they learn more, their utterances become more complex. They use these more complex forms because they need them to convey what they mean. As children acquire more vocabulary, they start to combine words, add inflections (e.g. *–ing* and *–ed*) and function words (e.g. *the*, *of*, *in*), and acquire constructions that go with the words they know. As a first step in elaborating their utterances, they move on from single-word utterances to combinations of words, as in the following two-word English utterances:

sit bed	(child wanting to sit on the bed)
fall book	(child reporting having dropped a book)
daddy sock	(child reporting that the father put on the child's sock)

But two-word utterances can be hard to interpret, even in context. *Daddy sock* could mean 'that's daddy's sock', 'daddy is putting on socks', 'that's a big sock', or the meaning apparently intended on this occasion: 'daddy is putting on my sock'. The interpretation of two- and three-word combinations generally depends on what the adult already knows about the setting and the child's intentions or routines – the common ground adult and child share at that point in the exchange.

Listening to utterances like these out of context makes the problem of interpretation particularly salient.

The kinds of word-combinations children produce at this stage are very similar, regardless of the language being acquired. For languages as different as Luo (Kenya), Finnish, English, Hebrew, Polish, Japanese, Samoan, German, and Hungarian, young children produce very similar utterances. One way to characterize such utterances is with the roles in the target event that the words pick out. In *daddy sock*, for example, *daddy* picks out the *agent* (the person putting on the sock) or, in another context, the *recipient* (the owner of the sock). In *sit bed*, the word *bed* identifies the location involved, and in *fall book*, *book* identifies the *object* affected by the action. Other roles include *experiencer* (<u>the man</u> heard the bang), *instrument* (*they opened the door <u>with a key</u>*), and locative *source* (*the dog came <u>out of the kennel</u>*) and *goal* (*the cat stalked <u>into the house</u>*). Identification of such roles in an event allows us to sort utterances into types and establish parallels across languages. Some combinations consist of an adult noun plus verb, others of two nouns, and others still of combinations containing deictic terms like *there* or *that*, or quantifiers like *more* combined with a noun or verb. Consider some typical two-word utterances from several languages:

Luo (Kenya)	Finnish	English
en saa 'it clock'	*vettä siinä* 'water there'	*that ball*
adway cham 'i-want food'	*anna Rina* 'give Rina'	*more milk*
omoyo oduma 'she-dries maize'	*talli bm-bm* 'garage car'	*hit ball*
kom baba 'chair daddy'	*täti auto* 'aunt car'	*mama shoe*
piypiy kech 'pepper hot'	*torni iso* 'tower big'	*big boat*
bede onge 'knife gone'	*ei susi* 'not wolf'	*no wash*
	missä pallo 'where ball'?	*where ball?*

German	Russian	Samoan
buch da 'book there'	*Tosya tam* 'Tosya there'	*Keith lea* 'Keith there'
bitte apfel 'please apple'	*day chasy* 'give watch'	*mai pepe* 'give doll'

puppe kommt 'doll comes'	*mama prua* 'mama walk'	*tapale 'oe* 'hit you'
mein ball 'my ball'	*pup moya* 'navel my'	*paluni mama* 'balloon mama'
milch heiss 'milk hot'	*papa bol'shoy* 'papa big'	*fa'ali'i pepe* 'headstrong baby'
kaffee nein 'coffee no'	*vody net* 'water no'	*le 'ai* 'not eat'
wo ball 'where ball'?	*gde papa* 'where papa'?	*fea Punafu* 'where Punafu'?

Children use two-word utterances like these to name or locate things, as in *there book*; to request things, as in *more milk*; to describe events, as in *hit ball*; to indicate possession, as in *mama dress*; to modify or qualify, as in *big boat*; and to negate or to question, as in *allgone cookie* and *where cup?* The functions of these two-word utterances appear to be remarkably similar across languages in children's early speech.

Formulaic utterances

Children pick up a number of fixed routines (e.g. /sæt/ '(what)'s that?') that they use, usually in appropriate contexts, for some time before they unpack the formulaic phrase and analyse its constituent parts – here: *what, is, that.* As we saw earlier, parents use a number of highly frequent, routinized or formulaic phrases to accompany many of the daily activities children participate in, whether changing diapers, getting dressed, getting into (or out of) high chairs at the table, meal times, nap times, bath times, greetings for arrivals and departures, and so on. Children pick up particularly frequent phrases to use, and it takes them some time to analyse the contents of each 'slot' in a phrase like *cup of tea*. It is only then that they realize that they can also say, when warranted, *cup of milk*, or *cup of soup*. In much the same way, they also tend at first to produce just one determiner with each noun: *the telephone, a biscuit, that book*, and it may take them several weeks or even months before they also produce those nouns – *telephone, biscuit,* and *book*, say – with another determiner, as in *that book, my book, a book*.

Formulaic utterances also act as carriers for irregular word forms, sometimes in the lines of songs or rhymes like *'Three blind mice'*.

Indeed, at an age when children over-regularize the plural forms of irregular nouns, constructing regular plurals for nouns like *mouse, sheep,* or *foot* in the form of *mouses, sheeps,* and *foots,* they *can* in fact produce the conventional irregular form when it occurs as part of a formulaic phrase. Four-year-olds, for instance, produce the conventional plural form *mice* when prompted with a specific frame like *Three blind —,* about 70 per cent of the time, compared to producing that form correctly only 30 per cent of the time when, for example, shown a picture of some mice and asked what they are. That is, the predictability associated with frequent frames facilitates children's retrieval of the appropriate form from memory.

This suggests that children may use such frequent collocations to help them establish the appropriate plural forms for nouns, mark the appropriate gender on articles and adjectives, mark case agreement on all the elements associated with a noun, and master irregular forms of various kinds that occur frequently in certain fixed frames.

Adding grammatical elements

Once children produce more than one word at a time, they elaborate the forms of their words. They add inflections to nouns to mark number (singular versus plural) and case (e.g. nominative for subjects, accusative for direct objects), and to verbs to mark number (e.g. *he* versus *they*), person (e.g. *I, you, she*), mood (e.g. *can, may, will*), aspect (e.g. completed, durative), and tense (present, non-present). These inflections tend to be acquired in an orderly fashion, but it takes several years for children to master adult-like paradigms of all the forms available for a particular noun or verb. It takes them several years to acquire all these morphological elements, most of them inflectional suffixes on the words children need to mark with number (singular versus plural) or case (several different suffixes depending on the role of each noun in the utterance). Inflections marked with prefixes are considerably rarer.

Children slowly build up sets of noun and verb forms (paradigms) by adding contrasting inflections and free-standing grammatical elements (called morphemes) like articles (*the*, *a*) and prepositions (*in, of, from*). To begin with, they produce a single form of a verb, in all contexts; this may be an inflected form, as in the English (past tense) form *fell*, but they simply use it initially for any event of falling. Then they add a second form of that same verb, let's say *fall*. In general this allows them to use a present tense verb form for ongoing actions, say (e.g. *break* or *breaking*), and a past participle for completed actions (e.g. *broken*). They also pick up ready-made, fixed sequences of article and noun, as in <u>the</u> book, <u>a</u> cup, <u>my</u> ball, and initially produce those nouns only with that determiner. That is, grammatical morphemes like *the* or *of* (these grammatical morphemes are also called function words), just like children's first inflections, appear initially in fixed combinations only, with particular nouns and verbs. Only later do children analyse such sequences and begin using nouns, say, with different determiners (*the book, my book, a book*) and verbs with different modals (<u>can</u> jump, <u>will</u> go) or different subject pronouns (<u>you're</u> going, <u>he's</u> going).

With nouns, children also typically start with a single form – only singular (*door, ball, spoon*) or only plural (*cups, blocks*), regardless of context or of the number of items actually being referred to. Later on, they begin to mark plural number on nouns when they talk about more than one entity, but they may not rely at first on the conventional way to do this, instead using a construction that combines a numeral like *two* and a (singular) noun, for example, as in *two frog* for several frogs, or using a quantifier like *more*, as in *more cup* for several cups on the table, or using reduplication, as in a sequence like *ball ball* for several balls. Children also take time in learning how to assign case endings appropriately in case-marked languages like Polish, German, or Finnish. Cases mark the roles in each event by adding a different ending to each noun. For example, the agent of the action generally gets the nominative case ending, the recipient of an action gets the dative case ending, and the object affected by the action gets the accusative case ending.

Two-word combinations and early uses of some grammatical morphemes are just the first step here. Children soon construct longer utterances. For example, a two-word combination like *Mummy read* might be elaborated as *I want Mummy (to) read* or later still, *Mummy, will you read that book?* Any phrase containing a noun can be elaborated with the addition of a demonstrative (*that* book) or a numeral and plural inflection (*two* book*s*), then modified further with adjectives and quantifiers, as in such referring expressions as *the small dog*, *two brown dogs*, or *some of those dogs*. Children expand their utterances because they need to, to make themselves clear.

Children at this stage also work on verb constructions, gradually adding modal and auxiliary verbs, as in *Molly will go*, *Tom has jumped the ditch*, or *Theo is watching the mouse*. This allows them to be more specific about the timing of an event – anticipated, ongoing, or already completed. They acquire more complex constructions with intransitive verbs, as in *Ian ran outside* (intransitive verb with a locative adverbial), *Lila is jumping in the puddle* (intransitive verb with a prepositional phrase); also with transitive verbs like *catch* and *stroke*, in *Sophie will catch the ball* (direct object), and *Emi wants to stroke the cat* (complement construction). Later, in order to keep track of which entity they are referring to, they add relative clauses to modify noun phrases, as in *Duncan saw the cat that was on the windowsill*. They add adverbial clauses to modify verb phrases, as in *Mimi climbed up the tree where the bird's nest was*, and they talk about a series of events while keeping track of their order, as in *They came in when they heard the bell ring*.

Languages differ, of course, in the properties children have to acquire. In English, German, and Mandarin, children must attend to word order. In English, this makes all the difference: compare *The dog chased the cat* and *The cat chased the dog*. In each utterance, the first noun phrase picks out the agent of the action (the one responsible for the act of chasing), while the second picks out the entity affected (the one being chased). In languages that use word order to mark grammatical relations, agents tend to be placed before objects-affected, and animate entities before inanimate ones.

Specific constructions may require special word orders, though, as in the resultative construction in English. This construction conveys the result of the activity denoted by the verb, with the resultant state expressed as the final element(s) in the utterance, as in *Landon wiped the table clean* (where the adjective *clean* denotes the end state) or *Chloë built her blocks into a tower* (where the prepositional phrase *into a tower* denotes the result of Chloë's action). The word order here marks the grammatical relations of subject, verb, and object, and the final state. In languages with case marking, speakers don't need to rely on word order to mark grammatical relations since the case marking on the noun indicates whether it is the subject (usually the agent) or the direct object of the action.

Languages commonly exhibit preferred word orders in adding modifications to noun phrases or verb phrases. For example, in English, adjectives precede their nouns, as in *the old castle* or *the shiny beads*, while in French and Spanish, most adjectives follow their nouns, as in *le papier jaune* 'the paper yellow = the yellow paper', or *la casa roja* 'the house red = the red house'. Consistency in the placement of modifiers, of course, makes it easier for speakers to process the information involved. This applies to other kinds of modification too, such as an added prepositional phrase, as in *l'homme au chapeau* 'the man with the hat' or an added relative clause, as in *l'homme qui porte le chapeau* 'the man who's wearing the hat'. Learning the constructions available allows children to understand others' intentions more easily and allows them to express their own intentions more clearly.

Keeping track of word order is important not only for adding inflections to nouns and verbs, generally placed at the ends of those words, but also for other grammatical elements like determiners (*the, a, that*) and quantifiers (*two, some*) added to nouns, and modals (*can, will, may*) and auxiliaries (*be, have*) added to verbs. In fact, children rarely or never make errors in where they add an inflection or a functional element in relation to a noun or verb form. This suggests that they attend closely to how things are ordered in the ambient language.

In languages with extensive case marking, word order plays a smaller grammatical role, and speakers use word order flexibly to convey the information flow, from information that is given to information that is new, within the utterance. The order chosen by the speaker marks what is currently given information, hence already known to the speaker and addressee (and in common ground), and what is new, with the latter generally placed at the end of the utterance. Consistent use of 'given before new' ordering makes it easier to process each utterance during a conversational exchange. As one might expect, children appear to use more variable word order in case-marked languages. This, of course, is what they hear from the adults around them.

Verbs and verb forms

Children produce verbs first in one single form, used in all contexts, for all persons. Only later do they add the relevant inflections and other grammatical elements that signal such things as person (first, second, third), number (singular versus plural), and tense (present versus non-present). In using verbs, they also tend to use them for talking about their own actions first, with no explicit subject, and only later extend the verb to talk about an action done by someone else. And they add subjects to indicate who the agent is.

When children's verbs are grouped into classes based on their general meanings in terms of the event types they refer to, it's clear that children attend to just such dimensions as they build up their verb paradigms. They distinguish four groups of verbs. The first group consists of verbs for *activities* (e.g. *run*, *walk*, *eat*), that in English commonly appear with the *–ing* ending. These refer to actions that can be extended over time. A second group is comprised of verbs for *accomplishments* (e.g. *open*, *break*, *give*) where the action results in a change of state caused by some agent. These verbs are produced early on in past tense form, typically quite a bit earlier than the past tense forms of verbs from the other three groups. A third group is made up of verbs for *achievements* (e.g. *begin*, *finish*) where the action is viewed as either just beginning, or as just ending. The last group consists of verbs that refer to *states* (e.g. *want*, *hear*, *feel*). In English, these verbs generally appear with the simple present (*he wants*, but not *he is wanting*).

Why do children attend to these distinctions early on? They attend to patterns of use in adult speech. First, adults favour certain inflected forms with certain verb types and produce them frequently when talking with children. They frequently use activity verbs with the *–ing* ending, whether in the present (*he is running*) or non-present (*he was running*). And they frequently use accomplishment verbs with a simple past tense form (*he open<u>ed</u> the box, she <u>broke</u> the window*). These patterns in adult speech appear to account for children's early acquisition of *–ing* forms with activity verbs and of *–ed* forms with accomplishment verbs in English. Note that children acquiring Italian also produce past tense forms first with accomplishment verbs. In short, preferences for certain verb forms with specific types of verbs in adult speech lead to earlier acquisition of those forms in children.

When children produce bare (uninflected) verb forms in single-word utterances, it is often hard to tell what meaning they intend. Adults often offer reformulations that interpret and expand such bare verb forms by taking into account what is going on in context. For example, adults pay attention to whether the action is being anticipated (future) or has already happened (past). This kind of feedback may be critical for children acquiring French where the infinitive and the past participle of many verbs sound identical, e.g. *sauter* 'to jump' and *sauté* 'jumped', are both /sote/ phonetically. But when a child holds a little doll on the edge of the table and says /sote/, parents take the utterance as anticipating jumping and will say something like *il va sauter* 'he's going to jump' or *il veut sauter* 'he wants to jump', using constructions that clearly indicate that the verb here is an infinitive, not a past participle. When the action has already taken place (with the doll on the floor), though, they say instead things like *il a sauté* 'he jumped', indicating that the action has been completed, using a construction with an auxiliary verb plus past participle. That is, adult reformulations here supply an interpretation for these early verb forms in the course of checking on the child's intention. Such checking-up offers valuable feedback that can guide children to analysis and understanding of the different meanings of verb forms that happen to sound alike.

Noun classes

In many languages, each noun has a gender: masculine or feminine in French; masculine, feminine, or neuter in German; common or neuter in Dutch. The gender affects the choice of a definite or indefinite determiner: <u>un</u> *livre* (a-masc book-masc), <u>la</u> *porte* (the-fem door-fem). It also affects the choice of adjectival form: *un livre* <u>*vert*</u> (a-masc book-masc green-masc), *la porte verte* (the-fem door-fem green-fem). Such agreement patterns show which words and grammatical elements are treated as a unit – here for instance, the referring expression *la porte verte* 'the green door'.

How do children learn to assign gender in a language? In many languages, for a small number of nouns, there is a match of sex to gender, with most terms for males being masculine, and most for females being feminine. But there are exceptions. In some languages, the form of each word can indicate whether it is masculine or feminine: in Spanish, nouns in final –*o* are masculine, and those in final –*a* are feminine. (Again, there are some exceptions, and some nouns end in consonants.) In French, there are some systematic differences in the sound patterns of distinctively masculine versus feminine noun endings, and children make use of these by age 4 to 5. What about earlier? When young children use the wrong gender, a wrong determiner like *la* for *le*, say, or a wrong adjectival form, as in *vert* for *verte*, or when they omit a determiner altogether, they generally get feedback from adults who supply the right forms as they check up on what their children mean. And children are continually exposed to adult usage, for frequent and infrequent nouns alike. Here again, frequent collocations in adult speech – phrases containing particular nouns – presumably help: children can start with whole phrases and only later analyse them into determiner plus noun. This way, the gender of each noun is marked by the determiner that co-occurs with it, as well as by any word endings specialized for masculine or feminine gender. Gender assignment appears easier for children with diminutive nouns in some languages, perhaps because diminutive nouns in Russian or Czech, for example, are all marked in the same way for gender.

Children face a similar problem in identifying case endings, the noun inflections that mark subjects, usually agents, and such roles as direct objects affected by the action (patients or themes), instruments, recipients, possessors, and locations. Case inflections in case-marking languages are often marked on determiners as well as on any adjective that modifies a noun. To complicate things further, in languages like

Russian and Polish, the set of case inflections varies with the gender and number of the noun, so singular and plural case endings for the same role typically differ. Learning all the case inflections for such a system takes a long time, and children often opt for partial generalizations along the way, making the language more regular than it actually is. With continued exposure and feedback, though, they have usually mastered the conventional system between age 6 and 8.

How long this takes depends on the internal regularity of the language. In studies comparing Hungarian and Serbo-Croatian, for example, children learn Hungarian inflections earlier than Serbo-Croatian ones. (The comparison was made with bilingual children.) Hungarian, like Turkish, presents children with a highly regular system, where each inflection carries a specific meaning and takes essentially the same form on every noun. In Serbo-Croatian, much as in Russian and Polish, the case endings for the same meaning differ in form with the gender and number of the noun, and also co-occur with prepositions that can take two distinct cases, each for a different meaning, e.g. 'at' versus 'towards'. This kind of complexity takes children longer to master.

Languages differ in how they mark grammatical relations – the subject and direct object of a verb, say. Some rely on case marking alone; some rely on word order alone, and some rely on a mixed system – some case marking combined with prepositions or postpositions, plus certain word order preferences. Children encounter complexity and simplicity (aka regularity) in different domains in languages, and this generally accounts for the path they follow in the acquisition of each language.

Summary

The first constructions children work on are those immediately relevant to the nouns and verbs they have begun to produce. They often begin with formulaic chunks, sequences adopted from adult speech without analysis into the nouns, verbs, and smaller elements like word endings and articles (*a, the*). They may use relatively fixed forms with some nouns and verbs, and, for example, invariably use *the* with certain nouns and *a* with others, or always use some verbs in imperative form (*give me . . .*) or with a first-person subject (***me** do it*). And they produce many early combinations with one 'fixed' term and one variable, as in *more book, more juice, more run*, and so on. These early constructions then give way to more elaborate forms.

Children start to use noun phrases with a consistent determiner-plus-noun structure; they add contrasting case endings in languages that use case marking; and, later on, they also add adjectives and other kinds of modification to their noun phrases (see also Chapter 6). They do much the same with their early, relatively 'bare' verb forms: they add inflections to mark person, number, aspect, and tense; they add modal and auxiliary verbs; and, for some languages, they add clitic subjects (pronouns that act rather like an added prefix on the verb).

All this makes children's utterances more intelligible because more of the relations between the nouns and verbs in their utterances are now explicit, but children still have a long way to go before they master still more complex constructions in their language. We now turn to these and why children need them.

Chapter 6

More elaborate constructions

Children's first constructions emerge as they combine two or more words, then add inflections to nouns and verbs, such as plural *–s*, or continuing activity *–ing*, along with some grammatical morphemes such as *the*, *it*, and *in*. They begin to use the transitive construction, where the agent noun appears as the subject (S), followed by the verb (V), and a direct object (O), as in *Alistair threw the ball*. For intransitive verbs, though, they combine subject and verb, SV, and may add an adverbial phrase as in *Kate ran into the garden*. Immediately after beginning to combine words, children start to acquire the inflections and function words that help specify the meanings of constructions. The acquisition of constructions goes hand-in-hand with the acquisition of (a) verbs and nouns for specific 'slots' in constructions (here, SVO and SV), and (b) the grammatical elements that show how the nouns are related to the verb in each instance. For example, presented with a familiar verb (*feed*) and an unfamiliar noun (*ferret*) as in 'Mommy feeds the ferret', children aged just 2 readily select a picture of an animal (a ferret) out of four pictures shown. That is, they use their knowledge of the meaning of *feed* to infer which of four pictured objects would be an appropriate referent for *the ferret*, namely some kind of animal. These 2-year-olds nearly always choose an appropriate referent for each combination of a familiar verb and unfamiliar noun. They also show good retention of the new nouns a day later. In short, children make use of meanings they already know here, in making their inferences about unfamiliar words.

What motivates children to acquire more elaborate expressions and constructions in their first language? What other constructions do young children need? Two-word combinations can take them only so far in making their intentions clear. To do more, they need more vocabulary and more constructions. They need to be able to understand and ask questions; they need to be able to assert and deny claims about particular states of affairs. But both questions and assertions may be complex, so children must be able to interpret and respond to more complex language. We begin by looking at questions and at negation. In English these constructions are linked structurally: both depend on an auxiliary or modal verb to carry tense, as we will see.

Questions

Children acquire question constructions fairly early. They produce some *yes/no* questions early, sometimes before any word-combinations even. These questions are at first marked only with rising intonation, as in *Going?* or *Put?* Early *yes/no* questions rarely appear in canonical form, with inversion of the auxiliary verb and subject, as in *Are you going?* Instead, 1- and 2-year-olds tend to use just a verb alone, as in *Coming?* (= Are you coming?), or a noun alone, as in *Blanket?* (= Where's my blanket?), or a combination of the two, as in *Ride train?* (= Can I ride on the train?), with rising intonation, to signal that the utterance is a question. Only later do they add subjects and auxiliary verbs. And only later still do they master the canonical patterns of inversion for the subject and auxiliary verb, with the latter carrying tense, as in <u>*Did*</u> *he jump?* or <u>*Are*</u> *you eating?*

D (1;3.19, about to throw a ball down the stairs): *put ball?*
D (1;4.12, wanting his pyjamas removed): *get that off?*
D (3;8.1, of pyjama jacket): *can you untake this off?*

After that, some *yes/no* questions begin to appear in canonical, but not yet fully conventional, form, as in: *Did I saw that in my book?* Notice that there are three possible *yes/no* question constructions here – *Are you coming?*, *You coming?*, or simply *Coming?* All three are common in adult speech. Adults frequently omit both the auxiliary verb and subject in such questions, or omit just the auxiliary verb. These non-canonical forms are sometimes the commonest *yes/no* questions children hear.

Wh questions also emerge gradually, with children displaying some comprehension of *Where* and *What* questions around 1;6 to 2;0, and only later responding appropriately to *Who* questions, then *Why*, and *Which*, followed last of all by *When*. Comprehension here is well ahead of production, but children may rely mainly on the content words in each question to come up with some interpretation. In production, 1- and 2-year-olds tend to produce early *Wh* questions as unanalysed formulaic forms, such as:

/sæt/?	– interpreted as '[what]'s that?'
/sæt/ *called?*	– interpreted as '[what]'s that called?'
/sæt/ *go?*	– interpreted as '[where]'s that go?'

But the identification of any actual *Wh* word lies largely in the ear of the observer: children often fail to pronounce them. Indeed, the adult distinction between *yes/no* and *Wh* questions itself may not initially be present. When 1-year-olds are asked to repeat adult question forms, for example, they say only a verb or noun from the original, as in:

Louise (1;3):	*bow-wow go?*	(where did the bow-wow go?)
Daniel (1;9):	*mummy doing?*	(what is mummy doing?)
Jem (1;9):	*car going?*	(where is the car going?)
John (1;10):	*doing there?*	(what is he doing there?)
Paula (1;11):	*mouse doing?*	(what is the mouse doing?)

Even when 2-year-olds produce an initial /w–/ in their question, it is often unclear what the target question-word is. And 1- and 2-year-olds take some time to analyse formulaic sequences like /sæt/ into the distinct elements *what*, *is*, and *that*, or /wʌsɪsgɔ/ into *where's*, *this*, and *go*. Once they do this, they ask an increasing number of *What* questions (often *What that?* combined with a pointing gesture) to elicit labels for objects and actions. They also produce such *Where* questions as:

Where kitty?	*Where Mama boot?*	*Where me sleep?*
Where horse go?	*Where my mitten?*	*Where my spoon goed?*

Like *yes/no* questions, *Wh* questions in English also require inversion of the subject and auxiliary verb (*Where is he going?*). Children usually master this in canonical *yes/no* questions before *Wh* questions. While their first *Wh* questions emerge anywhere from age 1;6 onwards, they take two to three years to master the various types of *Wh* questions, with *When* emerging last, only at around age 4 to 5.

Negation

Constructions using negation in English are closely allied to questions. Both require knowledge of how the auxiliary carries tense, as in *She didn't answer* (compare *She answered*). Children's earliest negations tend to rely on *no*, produced as utterance initial or final, together with an echo of the adult's prior utterance, used to reject or oppose, as in *No mittens* (meaning 'No, I don't want mittens on'), or *No I see truck* (in response to 'Did you see the truck?'). Children also sometimes produce *not* with the same function, as in:

Colin Fraser (adult):	Will I read it or will you read it?
Eve (1;9):	*Eve read it.*
Colin:	Oh, Eve's going to read it.
Eve:	*not Fraser read it.*
Colin:	Fraser's not going to read it?
Eve:	*Eve read it.*

Alongside such rejections of others' proposals, children soon start to use sentence-internal negatives. Initially these tend to take the form of an auxiliary or modal verb with contracted *not*, e.g. *don't* or *can't*. These negative forms appear before children produce any positive auxiliary verbs (*do*, *be*) or modal verbs (*can, will, may*). Only after this do they acquire English internal *not* as a negation form.

(a) *D* (2;0.15, sliding down in his seat at table): *bye bye*.
  Mother: Bye bye D.
  D (as he pulled himself up again):   *I don't gone under the table*.

(b) *Father* (having just whistled): Can YOU whistle?
  D (2;1.26): *no I can't. I a boy*.
  (a few moments later): *I a boy, can't whistle*.

(c) *Mother*: Are you tired, Adam?
  Adam (2;6): *no, I don't want to sit*.

And they take considerably more time to master such negative forms as *Nobody has been in there, Neither of us saw that, Don't give him any more*, or *They never liked that*. For negations like these, they have to learn the meanings of terms like *never, no-one, nobody, nowhere*, as well as the relations between *some* and *any* in positive and negative utterances.

Modification of noun phrases

Children extend their uses of constructions as they add more words, such as adjectives, prepositional phrases, and relative clauses. Their aim in using these, for example, to an adult wearing a blindfold, is to distinguish between near-identical objects, e.g. a bear with a yellow ribbon and a bear with no ribbon, or a girl holding a pail and a dog, and a girl alone. Children aged 3, 4, and 5 rarely produce adjectives (as in *the yellow bear* for the bear wearing a yellow ribbon), but they do use prepositional phrases (as in *the boy on the cow, the girl with the dog*) by at least age 3. And by age 5, they also use some relative clauses introduced with *that* and, later on, with *who*.

Early relative clauses generally lack any relative pronoun: children simply juxtapose two clauses, as in:

(a) D (1;11.22, showing off a cookie he'd been given): *look <u>I got</u>!* [look what . . .]

(b) D (2;0): *I see /ə/ building <u>Eve go</u>.* [. . . building where . . .]

(c) D (2;0.1, picking up his doll): *here /ə/ doll <u>Shelli give D</u>.* [. . . doll that . . .]

(d) D (2;0.9): *Herb work ə big building <u>have /ə/ elevator 'n it</u>.* [. . . building that has . . .]

(e) D (2;2.5, after deciding he'd heard a truck, not a car, outside): *I go outside see /ə/ truck <u>may have dirt in it</u>.* [. . . truck that . . .]

Children gradually come to add relative pronouns like *that*, *who*, and *where* (but don't always get them quite right):

(a) D (2;4.19, of a toy): *I'm going to show you <u>where Mr. Lion is</u>.*

(b) D (2;5.16, touching a wet spot on the front of the newspaper): *that paper <u>what Eve got</u> fell into a tiny puddle*.

Notice that young children add relative clauses after main clauses, and so avoid interrupting the main clause. When they are asked to repeat relative clauses, they tend to break them into two clauses coordinated with *and*:

Adult model	**Echo's version (2;2)**
(a) Mozart [toy bear] <u>who cried</u> came to my party.	→ Mozart came to my party.
	→ *Mozart cried* and he came to my party.

> (b)   The owl <u>who eats candy</u> runs fast.   → *Owl eat a candy* and he run fast.
> (c)   The boy <u>the book hit</u> was crying.   → Boy the crying.

This suggests they find it easier to understand relative clauses introduced with an explicit relative marker like *that*, *who*, *where*, or *which*. When there is no relative marker in English (as in *The boy the book hit left*), 2-year-olds find it difficult to discern the boundaries of the relative clause, and are unable to offer any coherent interpretation.

Number and quantification

Children grasp the distinction between one and more-than-one long before they master the conventional system for marking plurality in their language. How do we know that? Young children often make use of other forms early on to mark 'more-than-one'. One option in English would be to use a term like *more*, as in *more book*, but this is generally ambiguous between the meaning of 'another' and 'large quantity'. Another option would be to use reduplication, as in *book book* for more than one book. Yet another would be to use a numeral. The last option is one that many children choose before they master the conventional plural endings.

(a)   D (1;8.16, at the table, with a toy truck): *wheel.* (then pointing at a second wheel) *wheel two.* (then pointing at a picture on the milk carton) *cow milk.* (then back to the wheels on the truck again) *wheel two.*

(b)   D (1;9.14, playing with two doll-blankets he'd stashed in his chair): *one, one blanket.* (he then dropped one on the floor) *other blanket floor.* (then pulled the second blanket off the table and dropped it too; and, looking first to one side, then to the other, at the two blankets now on the floor) *two blanket.*

(continued)

(continued)

(c)   *Mother* (counting four frogs in picture): Look at these: one, two, three, four!
D (1;10.9): *frog, two frog.*

(d)   D (2;0.15, playing with his magnets, holding three or four in his hand)
Father: How many magnets have you got?
D: *two*!

This child began to use *two* as his plural marker with bare nouns at 1;8, and then slowly added plural inflections, noun by noun, with occasional overlaps in uses of *two* and the plural *–s* ending. By age 2;4, he stopped using *two* for plurals, and relied on plural suffixes instead, as in the words *books, frogs, cups, bibs*.

Knowledge of plural marking is distinct from knowledge about counting and count sequences. Two-year-olds can answer *What do you see* questions with nonconventional or conventional plurals for up to nine objects, but they manage *How many do you see* questions only for two or three objects (the limit of their ability to count). They do poorly with four or five objects and usually won't respond at all when there are six or more objects.

Quantifiers pose further problems: these often form part of a scale such as < *some ~ all* >, < *a few ~ more ~ most* >. (Other domains may be organized as scales too, as in the words for temperature: < *cold ~ warm ~ hot* >.) Children have to learn what membership in such a scale involves, and that use of one term from a scale implicates that the others do not apply. But first of all, they have to learn, for instance, what the quantifier terms mean, and while they may start with words like *more* (usually construed at first as 'some amount') rather early on, they may also spontaneously assign a quantifier meaning to a term that isn't a conventional quantifier:

(a)   D (2;0.13, carrying a lot of blocks): *D— have /ə/ spoonful block.*
Mother: that's an armful, not a spoonful.

(b)   D (2;0.14, displaying a handful of magnets): *D— have /ə/ spoonful magnets.*

(c)   *D* (2;1.15, carrying an armful of sticks): *I got /ə/ spoonful, I got /ə/ spoonful /ə/ sticks.*

(d)   *D* (2;1.26, planning to carry all his toys): *I reach it 'n get /ə/ spoonful my arm.* (with a gesture towards under his arm): *and then carry it upstairs.*

One problem in interpreting quantifiers is finding the appropriate set of contrasts. When told 'Some of the toys are on the table', adults infer that there are other toys not on the table: they compute a scalar implicature, where the speaker's use of *some* implicates 'not all'. Children often fail to make these inferences up to age 4 or 5, or sometimes older. One reason may be that they don't yet know that *some* and *all* are scalar alternatives, and that they must identify those alternatives in context when presented with tasks that require judgements about such terms as *some* versus *all*.

When 4-year-olds are given statements like 'Only some of the animals are sleeping' (when all the animals pictured are sleeping), they fail to reject them. But if instead they hear 'Only the cat and the dog are sleeping' (when all the animals pictured are sleeping), they correctly reject the description. So making the alternatives explicit helps children decide whether uses of *some* and *all* are true or false. They need to access the alternatives relevant to each context in order to identify the contrasting options. This in turn presumably helps them establish the conventional adult meanings of quantifiers and how they line up as members of various scales like < *none ~ some ~ all* >, < *some ~ more ~ most* >, < *none ~ part ~ all* >, as well as in other lexical scales like < *small ~ big ~ gigantic* >, or < *cold ~ warm ~ hot ~ scalding* >. This all takes time.

Place and time

Children begin to talk very early about place – the location of an event or the goal of motion in space. They use deictic locatives, *here* and *there*, in their earliest word combinations, usually with pointing gestures, to show where something is or where an event happened. And they talk about goals of motion, as in *outside, in the box, on the table.*

They regularly encode the path to a goal, and do so across a broad range of verb types, including manner-of-motion (*run* to a goal), change-in-possession (*give* to the new possessor), change-of-state (*turn red*, enter the new state), and attachment events (*put, stick* to some place). As young as 12 months, children show a preference for attending to goals when they see both sources and goals of motion. This finding suggests that there is a conceptual asymmetry in motion, such that children (and maybe adults too) represent goals as more salient than sources.

Their early expressions of source appear to be linked to their notions of agency (the agent or doer of an action), possession (the possessor), cause (of some effect), and comparison (the standard):

Agents and natural forces

(a) *D* (2;2.3, looking at pieces of sandwich he'd pushed off his plate): *this fall down from me.*

(b) *J* (2;2, of a visit to the doctor): *I took my temperature from the doctor.*

(c) *D* (4;6.9, commenting on a story): *Daddy, the pigs have been marooned from the rain.*

Cause, possession, and comparison

(d) *D* (2;6.13, remembering an earlier event): *then I cried a bit from you go get him.*

(e) *A* (3;0): *I see boats from Mommy.*

(f) *D* (2;8.15, of his car seat): *this seat is getting too small from me.*

Children make relatively little direct reference to time early on, but understand utterances like *Put on your socks and then your shoes*, and produce temporal expressions like *I paint <u>and then</u> I pick them up*, at around age 2;6 to 3. In comprehension, children pay attention to two factors: order of mention, where they treat the first event mentioned as the first event to have occurred, and clause order, where they prefer to place the main clause before any subordinate clause. As a result, 3-year-olds make some consistent errors when they act out instructions such as: 'The boy jumps the fence after he pats the dog' (with event-2 described before event-1), compared with their error-free acting-out of: 'Make the boy jump the fence before he pats the dog' (with mention of event-1 followed by event-2). Where the order of mention matches the order of the events in time, 3-year-olds make no errors, as with the instructions that begin with an *after*-clause (*After the boy jumps the fence, he pats the dog*) or a main clause followed by a *before*-clause (*The boy jumps the fence before he pats the dog.*)

By age 4, children latch on to the meaning of *before*, and begin to get instructions with both initial and final *before*-clauses correct, while persisting with an order-of-mention strategy with instructions that contain *after*-clauses. Not until around age 5 do children get both sets of instructions right.

When asked questions about when one of two events happened, younger children (here, aged 3) often fail to answer or give identical answers to questions about the first and second event, e.g. *now, just now, a minute ago*. When this is followed up with further questions: 'What happened first?' and 'What happened last?', 3- and 4-year-olds manage to answer nearly all the *first*-questions, but not the *last*-questions. And a few children at this stage give only locative answers to *when*-questions: *here, right here*. Among 4-year-olds who understand *before* but not *after*, there is an asymmetry in their answers to *when*-questions: they answer appropriately when they can use *before*, but have great difficulty giving any answers with *after*. One solution that a few children adopt is to rely on order of mention and simply list the events in order, e.g. in response to a *when*-1 question, they answer 'event-1 and then event-2', and in answer to a *when*-2 question, they give 'event-1 and THEN event-2'.

In short, like adults, children treat order-of-mention as reflecting chronological order for sequences of events, as in *They set up the tent and they climbed the tree*. This preference is modified as children master conjunctions like *when, before, after*, and, later, *while, until*, and *during*, which allow for descriptions that are 'out of order'. Their progression to more adult-like usage here begins around age 4, and they may take until age 6 or even later before their usage becomes stable.

Causation and cause

Children rely on verbs to express causation first. They turn intransitive verbs like *go* and *fall* into transitive causative verbs by adding a direct object, as *I'm gonna fall this on her* (meaning 'I'm going to drop this [paper] on her') or *I'm singing him* (meaning 'making him sing'). For some verbs in English, the intransitive and causative forms are different, e.g. *fall* versus *drop*, *eat* versus *feed*, *learn* versus *teach*, *come* versus *bring*, but many verbs differ only in the number and type of argument, with the intransitive versus causative forms of the verb itself being identical, as in verbs like *open*, *walk*, *sit*. Children as young as 2 also readily form new causative verbs from nouns:

(a) *S* (2;4, wanting some cheese to be weighed): *you have to scale it first.* [= weigh]

(b) *S* (2;7, having hit his baby sister who cried): *I broomed her.* [= hit with a (toy) broom]

(c) *S* (2;11, not wanting his mother to sweep his room): *don't broom my mess.*

(d) *S* (3;0.21, watching a man open a door with a key): *he's keying the door.*

(e) *S* (3;2, asking whether his pants are mended): *is it all needled?*

(f) *EB* (3;10, using tongs to take spaghetti out of a pan): *I'm going to pliers this out.*

(g) *CB* (4;0, rejecting some paper she'd cut her finger on earlier): *I don't think I'll have this because it papers me.* [= paper cuts me]

Some novel verbs fill gaps where there is no conventional verb available, but others should be pre-empted by the existence of a conventional lexical verb with just the intended meaning, e.g. *drop* for 'cause to fall', *sweep* for 'clean with a broom', *unlock* for 'open with a key', *chop* for 'cut up with a hatchet', and so on.

While adults typically offer feedback in the form of a conventional verb with the requisite meaning, some novel causative forms persist in children's speech even after they appear to have acquired the conventional verb. Conventional verb forms that are frequent in adult speech tend to replace the child innovations and errors earlier than infrequent ones, and those verbs where there is a single form that pre-empts the child's version appear to be mastered before less clear cases. Where child errors correspond to several different possible adult forms, children may well take much longer to sort out which form is the one they need on a particular occasion. Consider causative *stay*: it may correspond to *keep*, as in *Mommy, can you stay this* [= a door] *open?*, or to *leave*, as in *[she] won't stay things where I want them to be.* Similarly, causative *fall* corresponds both to *drop*, as in *I'm just gonna fall this on her*, and to *knock [down]*, as in *you fell me down.* And causative *go* corresponds variously to *take* (*go me to the bathroom*), to *send* (*do you have anything else you'd like to go to China?*), and to *put* (*go it over there*). Perhaps it is not surprising that, even with adult feedback, children continue to make some of these errors as late as age 12.

Children also attend to causal relations between events, and can describe these fairly early on as a cause followed by a result. That is, they follow chronological order in their order of mention, as in this 3-year-old's description of a causal sequence:

> *Alan* (climbing on some boxes): *I'll fall off and I'll jump* <repair> *I'll jump and I'll fall.*

While they begin with coordinate constructions in cause-effect order, once they shift to using a subordinate clause to describe the cause, they have to choose how to talk about a cause-result sequence. When they place the subordinate clause after the main clause, their order of mention no longer matches the chronological order, as shown in these utterances from 3;6-year-olds:

> *Nicola* (inside the playhouse): *they can't come here 'cos we're sweeping up.*
>
> *Steven* (wanting new paper on the easel): *take it off 'cos I'm going to paint on it.*

Next, children place subordinate clauses first in some constructions, as in:

> *Will* (constructing a garage from Lego): *when the train stops, this is where it goes.*
>
> *Maureen*: *when I was a baby, I got washed in a basin.*
>
> *Nicola*: *if wee Brian's naughty to me, I'll smack him.*

In causal sequences marked with *because*, children have two competing preferences: (a) use chronological order in their order of mention and (b) place subordinate clauses second. They must also take into account whether the effect or the cause comprises information that is given (versus new) in the exchange. Children, like adults, generally begin with what is given, and then add new information. But what is given may be the first of two events, or the second of two events. This makes a difference for the conjunction required. Attending to all these factors may well account for why children take several years to master causal constructions.

Conditionals and contingency

Children also use chronological order to express contingency between two events. Initially they use simple juxtaposition, as in some of their other early constructions, thus linking the contingent events, as in:

> *Kate* (2;4, climbing into her crib): *climb in. be fun.* (as she toppled in, laughing)

By age 2, children can distinguish actual from non-actual events, as shown clearly in their play (see Chapter 8), and they readily infer that specific events are connected. But conditional utterances take time to master: they are syntactically complicated because of the verb tense required for actual or future (generic) conditions (e.g. 'If it starts raining, I'll open the umbrella') versus hypothetical statements (e.g. 'If he came, everyone would be surprised', or 'If he had used the brakes, he wouldn't have hit the gate'). Certainty about the event that is anticipated also plays a role here: children learning English tend to use *when* for events that are certain (e.g. 'When Tom comes, we'll have a picnic') and *if* for events that are uncertain (e.g. 'If Tom comes, we'll have a picnic').

In short, children go through several stages in learning conditional constructions. At first, they juxtapose two clauses. Then they begin to use *when* and *if* for future predicted events:

(a)   *Adult*: What are umbrellas for?
      Lauren (2;7): when rain comes, we put an umbrella on top of us.

(b)   *Adult*: What if you fall in the water?
      Lauren (2;8): I'll get eaten by a shark.

(c)   *Amanda (2;11): when I older than Lindsey, then I'm the big sister.*

At this stage, they can produce some generic conditionals such as *If I eat too much, I get sick*, where they generalize about certain event-types. Their next step is to produce hypothetical conditionals, as in:

Ryan (2;10): if Bulldozer man saw a fire, he would call the fire department.

By age 4, they distinguish fact and supposition, and so differentiate their uses of *when* (certain) from *if* (uncertain) in conditionals.

(a)   *D* (3;6.14, appearing with his father's shoes)
      Father: Where were my shoes?
      D: *upstairs in the logs.* (= beside the fireplace)
      Father: I looked all over for them last night.
      D: *if you looked all over for them, you would have found them.*

(b)   *Grant (3;10): when I was <repair> if I was tiger, I would cook pa–<repair> popcorn.*

At this point, children make use of present, future, and hypothetical conditions where one event is contingent on another. But they still have to master the appropriate verb forms to use in each type of conditional construction, a task they may still be working on as late as age 11.

Summary

Children start out simply, using simple words to express simple ideas. But as they get older, they try to express more complex ideas, and for this they need more complex constructions. We see a clear progression in the questions children ask and answer as they acquire different question-word meanings and learn to offer appropriate answers, and in the different types of negation children produce as they start to use sentence internal negatives, with auxiliary and modal verbs, as well as with different negative terms. We also see advances in complexity in how children modify referring expressions with adjectives, prepositional phrases, and relative clauses in order to make their references clear.

Children display similar changes in complexity of expression as they work out how to distinguish 'one' from 'more than one', as well as in their specifications of place and time in their descriptions of events and of their order. And they progress to still more complex constructions as they talk about cause and contingency in events. In each domain, children add more and more elaborate constructions in order to express more complex ideas.

Chapter 7

Carrying on a conversation

What do children need to know to participate in a conversation? What does a conversation consist of? It might include exchanges of information, participants taking turns, use of referring expressions, responses to questions, and accumulation of common ground. Among other things, children need to identify adjacency pairs, pairs of utterances where the first calls forth the second, and so engages the other speaker. Candidate adjacency pairs include greetings, where each speaker contributes in turn (A: *hi.* —B: *hi*), questions, where the person questioned needs to answer (A: *When are you leaving?* —B: *At seven*), or offers where the person addressed must accept or reject the offer (A: *Would you like to come with us?* —B: *'fraid I can't this week*). In particular, with questions and answers, children need to identify different questions and the kinds of answer they each require. Compare a *yes/no* question like: *Do you want some toast?* with a *Wh* question like: *Where did you leave your gloves?* Speakers, here children, also need to get the timing of the second part of each adjacency pair right. And in the course of a conversation, they must maintain topics by adding new information in their turns. In this chapter, we look at how infants move from interaction with smiling and gaze to participating in conversational exchanges.

Interaction and communication

Well before they begin to talk, infants interact with adults, smiling, vocalizing, responding to gaze. And adults adapt, taking turns around what the infant does. By 9 or 10 months, infants begin trying to make others understand them. They point at things that attract their attention, and maintain their points until adults show that they have noticed. They reach towards things they want, and persist in reaching (often with a whining vocalization) until adults respond. When they achieve their goal, they drop their pointing or reaching gesture. This occurs when adults name or comment on what's pointed at, or make it accessible to the child, by lifting the child up to see better; or when they check up on what it is, exactly, that the child wants. Children also rely on demonstrating gestures, shaping their hand to 'hold' a cup near a jug of juice to request a drink, turning their head away from the spoon being tendered, or pushing away something offered that they don't want. And they rely on pointing or deictic gestures to answer certain questions, e.g. 'Where's your teddy?' or 'Which book shall we read?'

Children discover that gestures and preverbal vocalizations can be quite effective in communicating certain intentions. But these don't amount to having a conversation. For that, children need to do more. Once they can produce some words, they both gesture and talk as they play and carry on everyday activities. Conversations at the one-word stage, though, are hard to follow since children's words are not always recognizable, as in this exchange between Brenda, her mother, and a second adult, where Brenda first drew something she identified as 'wowow' (dog); she then tried to say *bone*, then switched to *Ralph*, the name of her cousins' dog:

Brenda (1;7.2):	/bəm . bəm . bam . bəu/
Mother:	Hm?
Brenda:	/boɪ̃ . boni . bəunĩ . boni/
Other adult:	Brown? Hm?
Brenda:	/ræuʃ . rous . rəuh/
Other adult:	Ralph? Yes, Ralph is a dog.

Brenda consistently made strenuous efforts to be understood from the first, offering variants on her production of a word, and trying with other, related, words to get over her intention. She relied heavily on repetition with variations, and as soon as her interlocutor gave evidence of recognizing the target word, would take another turn, as in this exchange about the fan:

Brenda (1;8, looking at electric fan): /fẽɪ̃ . fæ̃/
Mother: Hm?
Brenda: /fæ̃/
Mother: Bathroom?
Brenda: /fanĩ . faɪ̃/
Mother: Fan! Yeah.
Brenda: /kʰu/
Mother: Cool, yeah. Fan makes you cool.

In Brenda's earliest recordings (from 1;0.2 on), over two-thirds of her utterances were judged as unintelligible, but by age 2, adults recognized what she was trying to say around 85 per cent of the time. This improvement in intelligibility reflects her growing fluency in speaking. Children aged 2 are not only more fluent at producing single words; they can also combine words and add inflections and grammatical morphemes as well. Each of these steps makes them more intelligible. And, by around 2;6, they typically initiate more than half the conversational topics in adult–child exchanges.

As they learn more of the language, children go beyond the proto-assertions and requests exemplified by pointing and reaching gestures. They learn to make verbal assertions and requests, then how to promise and warn, how to express appropriate social reactions (*please, thank you, sorry*), and how to use language to perform certain actions (e.g. *you're it*) – all speech acts that speakers rely on as they communicate with others. These speech acts help speakers make their intentions clear, but there is no one-to-one mapping of utterance-types to speech acts. Speakers can assert with a statement: *Landon caught the ball*, or with a question: *Did you hear that Landon caught the ball?*, with a negative question: *Didn't you know that Landon caught the ball?*, and so on. And they can warn or threaten in many ways too: *I told you to leave that alone*; *Don't touch it or I'll tell Dad*; *If you touch that, I'll take your bike away* . . . Children's skill in identifying and using speech acts develops along with their language.

What topics do children propose with adults? They talk about the here-and-now, objects and events in everyday routines, objects they can handle and play with, like spoons, keys, blocks, toy cars, small action figures, dolls, and any activities they participate in. They engage in joint activities with adult caregivers: putting shapes into a shape-box, building towers with blocks, placing pieces in jigsaw puzzles, identifying objects and activities depicted in books, putting away toys, sorting spoons and forks. And they enact in their play many everyday routines: washing, dressing, going to sleep, eating. In doing all this, they talk about the objects and actions they are focussing on, and add new words as adults offer them, explicitly or indirectly, in the course of talking.

In early exchanges there is little talk about future events. Children focus initially on immediately-anticipated actions, e.g. a 1-year-old at the top of the stairs planning to throw a toy down, but first looking down and saying *uh-oh* with toy still in hand. Only later do they take up more distant events in the future, e.g. making plans for what to do at the beach. They also talk about the occasional past event, e.g. a 1;6-year-old saying *glass* while pointing to the empty windowsill where an adult had placed his glass the night before, or a 2-year-old saying *truck outside* to allude to the noise made earlier that morning by the garbage collectors. Most of their talk, at this stage, is about the present and what is visible in context.

Common ground

For conversations to work, the participants need to keep track of what they already know, and what is added in each turn in the exchange. This requires that they keep track of joint attention (are they each attending to the same thing?), physical co-presence (is the entity in joint attention physically present in the current context?), and conversational co-presence (is the speaker talking about or gesturing to that co-present entity?). These three conditions are essential to all communicative exchanges. Without them, speakers cannot establish common ground.

In conversation, speakers make use of common ground, ratifying each new piece of information added in the conversation, and so accumulating common ground during each conversation. In early conversations, children depend on their adult interlocutors already knowing about the topic that they initiate. This allows the adults to offer supportive scaffolding that enables very young children to talk about events at a stage when they are not yet capable of recounting an episode in narrative form, as in the exchanges cited earlier for D aged 1;6, startled when a friend's budgerigar landed on his head, or from Meredith, also 1;6, trying to tell the tale of her Band-Aid.

As children acquire more words and produce longer utterances, adults reduce the amount of scaffolding they provide. That is, as children's language skills expand, they gradually take on a fuller role in conversation, and become more skilled at establishing common ground. For example, if children are talking to family members, they take for granted knowledge of everyday routines, their house, toys, games, books, and so on. As they get older and their knowledge of language expands, so too does their potential common ground with other speakers of that language. As children add to their vocabulary, they assume that adults know the words for things and can provide them as needed. Children elicit words for unfamiliar objects and events by pointing and by asking numerous *What's that* questions. And adults offer new words when their children have either mis-labelled something or are being introduced to something new.

Child (2;11, looking at a book with Mother)
Mother: I don't know if you know what that one is.
Child: *that's a snake.*
Mother: It looks like a snake, doesn't it?
              It's called an eel. It's like a snake only it lives in the water.

Children learn how to establish common ground with new people – children and adults. And they become better at tracking what is and isn't in common ground. This may show up in what they know about using various elements of the language, for example the definite determiner *the*, as in:

(a) *Sarah* (3;6.6, with no prior mention): *where's the black tape?*
   Mother: What black tape?

(b) *Christy* (7;0.21, listening as younger sister Eva tells their mother about a TV programme, without any previous mention of an island)
   Eva (5;0): . . . . *the island.*
   Christy: *you're saying 'the'! . . . she doesn't know!*

In the exchange between the sisters, the older child Christy was quite aware that use of *the* called for information already in common ground, but Eva had not previously mentioned any island. Children over-use the definite article up to age 5 or 6, but since they show in many other ways that they track what the addressee knows from as young as age 2, or younger, such over-use suggests that children simply take a long time to learn how to use *the*, rather than any over-attribution of common ground.

Common ground requires that each participant be aware of specific information offered by a speaker to be ratified by another, with looking, touching, or repeating the word(s) said. Such forms of ratification offer a primary means of placing new information into common ground: they show that the current speaker has both heard and taken in the new information just offered. In fact, repeats of the word said by the child are common in adult-child conversations. There they serve two purposes: with repeats, adults both ratify and offer children a model of how to say that particular word, and children confirm that they have heard the word in question and try it out for themselves:

(a) *Hal* (1;10.26): *what's this?*
   Mother: It's a beaver.
   Hal: ***beaver**.*

(b) *Mother*: That's a wolf.
   Hal (2;0.14):   ***wolf**. like a big dog.*

> (c) *Child* (2;3): *red* /kændo/
>   *Mother:* **Red candle**.
>
> (d) *Child* (2;3): *that climbing.*
>   *Mother:* **That's** for **climbing** and it's called a ladder.

In each of these exchanges, the participants acknowledge a prior contribution by repeating part or all of it. In doing that, they put the information into common ground.

Given and new

In conversation, speakers keep track of what information is given (and so already in common ground), and what information is new. New information is generally tagged in English by utterance-final stress, or contrastive stress if it is not final, and by word order, with what is given generally followed by what is new within an utterance. Young children may rely on stress to mark new information in English before they rely on word order. Their reliance on stress here can be seen in children's monologues accompanying their own actions early on, as well as in some of their conversational turns:

> (a) *Seth* (1;9, playing and commenting): *man.* BLUE *man.*
> (b) *Seth* (1;9, playing): *ball.* NICE *ball.* ORANGE *ball.*
> (c) *Mother* (looking at picture book): What is the street?
>   *David* (2;5): FIRETRUCK *street.*

In utterances containing subject and object, children typically place stress on the object as new information. And in utterances containing object and location, the stress is nearly always on the location as new. Eventually, children learn to coordinate stress and word order to mark new information in English.

Turn timing

When talking to just one other person (an adult), even very young children are presented with turn-taking opportunities. Adult speakers wait for their children to say something, and only then take another turn. But as children participate in larger conversations, with a sibling and a parent, say, they have with a problem: others take turns faster than they do, so they may be closed out of the conversation. And where they have something to say, they end up saying it two or three seconds after it would have been relevant. The other speakers have already moved on.

Children have to keep track of when to contribute to a conversation and what to say. This means keeping track of other speakers and what they are saying. To do this, they must attend to timing. When adults talk, they take turns with minimal gaps (often 200–400 milliseconds or less) and with minimal overlap with the previous speaker. Children aged 1 and 2, though, may take up to three seconds to produce an answer to a question, and adults may judge the content of the child's next turn as relevant even when it comes over four seconds later. When do children learn to speed up enough to hold on to their turns at the appropriate point in an exchange?

Consider questions and answers: when children answer a question, they need to understand the question and simultaneously plan and initiate a response. And they need to learn how to anticipate when the current speaker's question will end, so they know when to start talking themselves. To do this, they must take into account both the content of the question – the words used – and the intonation contour used by the speaker. Words, though, may be the more important cue for younger children.

Questions and answers dominate in studies of turn timing for both adults and children. This is because a question and its answer form an *adjacency pair* – where the first of the two, the question, requires that the next speaker offer an answer as soon as possible, so as to maintain the exchange. In cross-linguistic studies of adult timing for answers to *yes/no* questions, researchers have found that in many different languages, speakers' modal answers are produced between 0 and 400 milliseconds after the end of the question. That is, with no perceptible gap and no overlap.

Anticipating when the current speaker's turn will end is one factor in coming in on time. Planning a response and executing it is another.

Children initiate simple answers (just one word or just *yes* or *no*) more quickly than complex ones (word combinations of various lengths), but they are considerably slower than adults in doing this. Their answers to *yes/no* questions show a steady increase in speed of onset from 1;8 to 3;5, when children get close to adult-like timing. For answers to *Wh* questions, the developmental picture becomes harder to assess because children master the meaning of each *Wh* word at different stages. Overall, children progress from single words to more complex answers to both *yes/no* and *Wh* questions as they get older. More complex answers, naturally, take more time to plan and produce. Children get faster at initiating more complex answers as they get older, once they have learnt more language and become better at using it.

In order to speed up in initiating answers, children have to anticipate the end of the prior speaker's turn. With questions they could attend to the form of the question and to the *Wh* word used, as well as to the content words, to get not only at the kind of information needed in the answer, but also at when the utterance is projected to end. Take a question like 'Where are your shoes?' Children could attend to the word *shoes* alone and look around for shoes, on the assumption that the adult is asking for shoes or something connected to shoes. Therefore, pointing at shoes, fetching shoes, or saying *there* (with a pointing gesture) or *shoe there* would all count as appropriate answers. They could also use the intonation patterns for *yes/no* (final rise) and *Wh* questions (slight final fall) to anticipate the ends of turns. Children, like adults, rely on both types of cue, with lexical information getting priority early on.

Consider the 'owl' exchange again. In the mother's first turn, she first mentions *birds*, then names the specific kind in question, namely *owls*. But the child's first 'acknowledgement' of this information lags behind a little: she acknowledges with *birds* only in her turn 2. And only after the mother has gone on to give the characteristic sound emitted by owls, does the child acknowledge the label *owls* (turn 3). And it is only after the mother reiterates the information about what the owl says, that the child takes up the sound, *hoo* (in turn 4). In each of these turns, the child comes in late, in the sense that if each turn were moved up one, it would provide a more immediate acknowledgement of what the mother had just said.

> *Child* (1;8.12, looking at picture of owls in new book): *duck. duck.* (turn 1)
> *Mother:* Yeah, those are birds. <looks at picture>
> They're called owls. <points at picture>
> Owls, that's their name. Owls. <looks at child>
> *Child:* **birds**. (turn 2)
> *Mother:* And you know what the owl says?
> <points at the picture again> The owl goes 'hoo'. 'hoo'.
> *Child:* **owl**. (turn 3)
> *Mother:* That's what the owl says.
> *Child:* **hoo**. <smiles> (turn 4)
> *Mother:* that's right.

As children get faster, they also make use of elements that signal they are about to take the next turn but are not quite ready: anticipatory *uh*'s and *um*'s followed by a pause, and the occasional *well* . . . They know by age 2 that they *should* take the floor as fast as possible after the other person stops speaking, and, that by signalling that they intend to do so, they can buy a little more time to plan their answer to the question.

Play and reality

Children talk during social play, so this offers another arena where they practise language and conversation. Some of this practice reflects everyday interactions on familiar topics as they play with parents and, later, with other children. Besides enacting conversational exchanges relevant to their activities, they enact different voices for different roles, and in addition manage what they will say, with 'stage directions'. As they develop collaborative play, they enact not only everyday experiences but also fictional episodes where they do the voices for different characters, and choose how to speak for specific roles. As they get older, they take into account age, gender, and status. And they switch roles, from the child playing, to a character inside the play, as when this 3-year-old places herself inside the play by speaking for the doll.

Mother and 3-year-old, playing with a dolls' house,

Mother: And then we can – shall we say that this is your room then?

Child: *yes.*

Mother: It's the Maja doll's room. That's what it is.
                  What furniture does the Maja doll want to have in her room?

Child (very squeaky voice)*:*   *I want to have the furniture in MY room.*

Two-year-olds collaborate with parents in play, taking on and assigning family roles (mother, father, child), as they have a pretend meal (with offers of food and drink); as they shop (what they buy and pay for); or as they put a doll to bed (undressing, bathing). This early play generally echoes various aspects of familiar everyday events. But as they get older, children start to differentiate the language used in each role. At 3 and 4 years old, children distinguish speech to mothers from speech to 1-year-olds: they use longer and more complex utterances to mothers, compared to significantly shorter utterances – with missing grammatical elements, routines like *There you are, You want more?*, and use of names in place of pronouns, as in *Becky want more?* (= you want more) – to babies and, to some extent, to peers. Besides more name use, they also use more repetitions and more imperatives in speech to babies. When they take the role of baby themselves, they use single-word utterances (*bottle*; *blanket*; *hat*; *milk*), simple combinations of words (*no touch*; *hat on*; *what dat?*), but also some utterances that are way out of the range needed, e.g. *Could you put my sweater on?* or *Oh, I'm just resting.* Their ability to act out fully age-appropriate speech is not quite there yet. These children distinguished how they talked to mothers from how they talked to peers or babies. In differentiating among their addressees, they made use of several features found in adult speech with children: shorter utterances, repetitions, frequent questions, names in lieu of pronouns, and so on.

By age 5, children are good at setting the stage for particular play episodes, doing the voices for particular roles, and giving stage directions.

The mix of these elements varies with the kind of play, from enactments with small figures as props for whom the children do the voices, to roles assigned to themselves and to other children in play episodes of varying length. They prompt (part of the stage directions) in a normal voice but sometimes with lowered volume; they offer background narrative, in third-person form, to set scenes. And they may start out with formal proposals like *Let's pretend . . .* or *Make believe that . . .* as they move from the actual kindergarten to the staged episode. In their play, even children as young as 3 or 4 distinguish stage directions, often in the past tense (in English, Dutch, and German, for example) or the imperfect tense (in French or Italian) from actual role-play, which is marked by the present tense:

Stage Directions

Dutch: *ik <u>was</u> de vader en ik <u>ging</u> een diepe kuil graven.*
          'I <u>was</u> the father and I <u>was</u> going to dig a deep hole'
English: *pretend turtle <u>found</u> it in the water.*
German: *dies ist ein Pferd und das <u>wäre</u> der Stall.*
          'this is a horse and that <u>would be</u> the stall'
French: *tu <u>étais</u> le gendarme et moi le voleur.*
          'you <u>were</u> the policeman and me the burglar'
Italian: *la porta <u>era</u> qui.*
          'the door <u>was</u> here'

That is, children distinguish non-actual play from reality as they plan and enact play episodes, and may allude to both in a single turn, as in this exchange between Jamie and a friend:

Friend (5;0):   <u>He bumped his tail</u>. *oh my tail.*
Jamie (5;6):   *wahwah. I've killed everything.*
Friend: <u>But you was wrong</u>. <u>Turtle was alive</u>.
         <u>*And you said:*</u> 'Ah, I'll cut your head off'.

In elicited talk for different roles, children display what they know about language. Children aged 4 to 7 are increasingly skilled in 'talking for' puppets in different roles in such settings as the family, the classroom, and the doctor's office. When asked to do the voices for two of three puppets in each scene (rotating across roles in elicitation sessions), these children distinguish their talk as-child (in the role of child) from talk as-mother or talk as-father. In the role of (small) child, they typically rely on high pitch, short utterances, and some omissions of grammatical morphemes. They differentiate addressees, using politer, less-direct requests (hints) to father (*Ice-cream tastes nice, doesn't it?*) than to mother (*Mommy, I want a drink of water*). As parents talking to child, they rely on hints (*Sweetie, time to wake up*) and imperatives (*Go home!*), but as-child talking to parent, they use statements of need (*I want a cookie*) and polite requests (*Would you take me home?*). They also differentiate the mother and father roles, but the contents of their utterances are largely based on stereotypes of what mothers and fathers typically do (even when this doesn't match their own family structure) – with mothers at home looking after children and cooking, and fathers going off to work with briefcases. Such stereotypes are discarded only as children get older, at around age 8 or so.

Children this age are less skilled at playing roles in a classroom setting where the roles are teacher, pupil, and foreign pupil. While they differentiate teacher and pupil in their language, with requests, for example, being politer in speech to teacher, they have a harder time distinguishing the native-speaker pupil from the foreign (limited English) one in the talk used for these two roles. The roles in a visit to the doctor typically involved talking, at various times, as child-patient, as-doctor, as-nurse, and as-one of the parents. Again, children distinguish among addressees, with talk to doctor being politer than talk to nurse, and talk to all adults politer than talk to child (child-patient). These children are clearly aware of age and status in each role.

Children also draw on whatever relevant vocabulary they know in each setting. In the doctor scenario, for example, children produce such terms as *temperature* and *thermometer*, *broken*, *cast*, *cut* (for 'operate'), *damage* (in the throat), *medical* (for 'medicine'), *stitches*, *shot-things* (for 'syringes'), *aspirin*, and *X-ray*. But they sometimes misjudge the words to use:

> *Child* (6;0, as-doctor): *I'll have to operate – scalpel, screwdriver, and uh, what else can we use?*

Play then is an opportunity for practice: for talking in a particular role (child, father, teacher, doctor), and for differentiating roles by age (as-mother versus as-child, as-teacher versus as-pupil), by gender (as-father versus as-mother), and by status (as-doctor versus as-child-patient). In doing this, children need to mark each speaker-role with appropriate choices of request-type: an imperative from a high status speaker to someone lower on the ladder, but a polite request (*Could you . . .*) from someone lower down to a high-status addressee. Children aged 4 to 7 consistently use politer requests when speaking as children to fathers than to mothers, and when speaking as-nurse to doctors, or as-pupils to teachers. They also begin to draw on specialized vocabulary for specific roles, even though their knowledge of the appropriate words is still limited. Their observation of social roles, visible in their enactments, shows what they have observed in the people interacting and talking with them.

Summary

Children's conversations with adults and with peers change as they get older. They have more to say and they become more skilled at talking to others. Adults offer them less and less scaffolding, and children become more skilled at assessing and at adding to common ground. In doing this, they also go beyond acknowledging new information offered by another speaker, and begin to contribute new information themselves, in their turns at talk.

Children also become more skilled at taking turns. Much of this depends on timing: 1- and 2-year-olds come in late. When they answer questions, they leave gaps between the speaker's question and the onset of their answer. But by age 4, they are approaching adult timing, and so become better able to make timely contributions and to add to common ground in multi-party conversations.

Children also become adept at producing speech that is appropriate for specific social roles. They have begun to attend to status and age in how people talk, in the kinds of requests they make, and to the kinds of vocabulary one might hear from different speakers. They distinguish the kind of speech appropriate for fathers, mothers, and small children, and for doctors, nurses, and child-patients. Some of the distinctions they can make in doing the voices for puppets that embody particular roles also turn up in their pretend-play as they take on various roles there. And in pretend-play, they are careful to distinguish their talk in play from any stage directions they use in setting up that play.

Chapter 8

Perspectives, viewpoints, and voices

When speakers choose their words for a referring expression, they are choosing the perspective they wish to present to their addressees. For example, a speaker might refer to a neighbour's dog as *the dog*, *the collie*, *that animal*, *the incessant barker*, or *my neighbour's pest*, under different circumstances. The referring expression chosen marks, to some extent, the perspective (and attitude) the speaker is taking at that moment towards the neighbour's dog. In another case, the speaker might refer to her neighbour as *my neighbour*, *the clarinettist*, *the children's music teacher*, or *that woman over there*, depending on which information would be most useful to her addressee in the context of the conversation. As speakers, we make use of this flexibility in language, and freely apply a variety of referring expressions to the same entity or category on different occasions. Each referring expression has a different sense (the meaning that marks the perspective chosen) but the same referent. This feature of language allows speakers considerable freedom in how they categorize entities and events linguistically for different addressees, in different settings, on different occasions.

When children hear multiple terms in referring expressions for the same entity or the same event, they must work out how these expressions differ in meaning, and why speakers use them. Lexical choice is just one element in perspective taking in language. Speakers also vary the grammatical form of the verb (this is often called the 'voice' of the verb). They may present an event in the active voice, as in *The boy lit the fire*, or they may omit the agent (*the boy*) and simply talk about the object affected by the action, in what is called the middle voice, as in *The fire lit quickly*. (This is not very common in English.) Or they may present the event, starting with the fire and mentioning the agent only after the verb given in the passive voice, as in *The fire was lit by the boy*.

Perspective can be marked with both lexical and constructional choices. Children must pay attention to both facets of perspective-marking as they work out how speakers use them. We begin by looking at when and where children master these aspects of conceptual perspective-taking, and then turn to how they exploit them in telling stories.

Lexical and constructional perspective

When children start using language, they too must choose their words and thereby characterize the objects and events they wish to talk about. On occasion, even early on, they may use two words to refer to the same thing, and do so in order to mark distinct perspectives on it. The extent to which this option is available depends, of course, on the size of their vocabularies and on their organization. This can change from day to day as children add new words and discover which old words can 'include' others because they are superordinates, e.g. *animal* (*dog, cat, lamb, zebra*), *toy* (*doll, teddy, block, ball*), *clothes* (*socks, scarf, jacket, hat*), *food* (*cereal, apple, cheese, cracker*) or because they offer orthogonal or overlapping categorizations, e.g. *fish/pet, lion/hunter, father/fireman*. Children build on their knowledge of physical space, where they understand, for example, that pictures and pages must be turned to *face* the relevant person if that person is to see what the child sees. This is apparent as early as age 2, when children can arrange toys in a parade, facing the direction of motion, and also explain what toys can 'see' from different positions:

> D (2;0.9, playing with two plastic rabbits and a small figure; D placed all three on a low table, along one edge so they faced his mother): /ə/ *watching Eve, rabbits watch Eve.* (then he moved them to an adjacent edge, turning them 90° to face his father): /ə/ *watch Herb.*
>
> *(continued)*

(continued)

Father: Can you make them watch television, can you make the rabbits watch television?

D: yes. (he rearranged them along another edge so they all faced the TV, and added some more toys, also facing the TV; then pointed at them): *Eve, Eve, /ə/ all watching TV.*

By age 2;6 or so, young children readily grasp that different referring expressions can be used for the same entity. *Peter* can also be both *the rabbit* and *the animal* on different occasions, depending on how the speaker wishes to present that individual to the current addressee, at the relevant level of categorization. Objects sometimes belong to two different domains, as when *the rabbit* and *the postman* refer to the same entity (as in Richard Scarry's books full of anthropomorphic characters) – rather than being linked hierarchically, as in *a rabbit is an animal*. Children aged 2 and 3 are good at answering questions that require two distinct labels and can readily designate a cat figure as *the cat* and as *the cook* on one occasion, and equally readily designate the same cat figure as both *the cat* and *the animal* on another.

(a)   *D* (1;7.20, naming each animal as he removed it from a puzzle): *lion. tiger. zebra . . .* (then, after doing the puzzle, with every piece back in place): *animal back.*

(b)   *D* (2;1.27, when his mother asked what he was usually called)
      Mother: Are you 'lovey'?
      D: *no, I 'Damon', I 'cookie', I 'sweetheart'! Herb 'lovey'.*

(c)   *D* (2;5.4, of wastebasket, always called 'basket' when he threw things into it, as he put it over his head): *that a hider. hide me in there.*

The ability to mark different perspectives on the same referent emerges early, at around age 1;6 or 2, as soon as children acquire enough relevant words. And they are exposed from the start to adults using different referring expressions for the same referent on different occasions: *the fruit* and *the banana*, *the dog* and *the collie*, *your cereal* and *your Cheerios*, *the bread* and *the sandwich*, *the house* and *the building*, *the whale* and *the beluga*, and so on. By age 4, children readily switch perspective and express this spontaneously in their talk as they consider different roles and views of the world:

> (a) D (3;11.17, in a wild animal park): ANTS *think people are walking trees.*
>
> (b) D (4;5.2, Mother reading Kenneth Grahame's *The Reluctant Dragon*; D holding his fingers 2 cm apart): *and I would be this big to the dragon.*
>
> (c) D (4;6.27, thinking about giants): *for a* GIANT, *a year is just an hour, and an hour is just a minute!* (pause) *and for an* ANT, *an hour is a year!*
>
> (d) D (4;9.2): *Mummy, a fork is like a rake to a mouse.*

Tracking viewpoints in others

Children attend to what their addressees know. For example, in a setting where parents watch another adult (the experimenter) hide something in a box out of reach, 2-year-olds simply point at the box to indicate where the object is that they want, but when their parents have their eyes shut or have been outside the room instead, 2-year-olds specify the location too, as in *that box*, *in that box*. They take account, in effect, of what their parents know by considering their physical viewpoint. Notice that taking someone else's *viewpoint* is not the same as taking their *conceptual perspective*. One can present different conceptual perspectives on an object from the same viewpoint, as when the child chooses *in that box* versus *in that container*.

Other viewpoint tasks present children with harder tasks: for example, they may observe (but not participate in) play scenes enacted with dolls where the experimenter narrates the action, and the children have to keep track of what each doll can see (that doll's viewpoint) and what that doll therefore knows about where some chocolate has been hidden.

The children are then asked questions like: 'Where will Maxi [name of doll] look for the chocolate?' When children are observers rather than participants in such scenes, they have difficulty keeping track of all the viewpoints involved and remembering who knows or who believes what. In effect, they have to keep track of their own as well as two or more other viewpoints as character-A hides something and as character-B then moves that object to a new location. The task for the child is then to say where A thinks the object is (i.e. A's viewpoint on the event just enacted), compared to where B thinks it is (B's viewpoint).

Observers in these tasks have a heavy memory load to deal with as they track three distinct viewpoints: their own as onlooker, plus those of A and B, along with the time-course involved as the object is moved from one place to another. Not surprisingly, 4-year-olds fail to keep track of who knows what by the end. (Adults are not very good at this either.) But when the task is simplified, for example by allowing children to keep track of just one character's viewpoint at a time, and simply asking children 'What will A do next?' (instead of 'Where will A look for X?'), many 3;6 year olds show that they can judge correctly what A believes about the location of the target object, by having A look in the relevant place.

Children as young as 2 *can* and *do* keep track of what another person thinks or believes. For example, when asked to hide something from a parent, and later being questioned about whether the parent knows where that object is, they answer, correctly, that the parent doesn't know. Being a participant in the action clearly helps.

Although keeping track of multiple viewpoints is hard, children can keep track of what someone else thinks, over and above their own viewpoint. This is evident not only in such viewpoint-tracking tasks, but also in how children attend to what their addressees do and don't know in particular contexts, and how they design their utterances to take that into account. Keeping track of viewpoint is also integral to pretend-play, and children keep good track of where they are at each moment. They use language from early on to distinguish 'play' from 'reality' in their talk (Chapter 7). Play itself generally requires ongoing shifts in viewpoint. In general, children attend to what is actually happening around them in the real world; in play, they are pretending, taking on particular roles (each with its viewpoint), and doing actions in a pretend world, like these two 3-year-olds:

A. Pretend this was my car.
B. No!
A. Pretend this was our car.
B. All right.
A. Can I drive your car?
B. Yes, okay. <smiles and moves away; A turns wheel and makes driving noises>

Play allows children not only practice in using language, but also practice in both taking and tracking different viewpoints.

Voices, roles, and identities

Children also need to take viewpoint into account as they do voices for different roles in pretend-play. As they shift from one role to another, they must keep track of what distinguishes the roles, and what characteristics they have assigned to each one as they talk in the role of child, father, teacher, or doctor, say, in particular settings. They learn to present different roles (each with a different viewpoint) by choosing language appropriate to each one. They differentiate the voices needed by changing pitch (higher for children, lower for men), choosing words and terms of address according to the role of the person speaking. They also choose utterance-types appropriate to their talk in each role. Their exposure to different roles and the experience they have had in observing them affects how well they carry all this off.

By age 4 to 5, children also start to construct their own identities, sometimes acting out possible scenarios and interactions, with a single child doing two voices, for example, as she works on how to present herself, how to act, or what to say in particular settings, in defining her own social role. The focus in such working out of social roles is often on disputes and negotiations among children, as in this dispute between two 6-year-old boys, A and B:

A: Give me that ball, you little . . .

B: No.

A: Give me that ball. <grabs ball>

B: You give me that ball back.

A: No.

B: You give me it. Give me that ball. <grabs ball>

A: Give it.

B: No.

A: Yes, I got it first.

B: I got the ball.

A: Give me it.

B: No, I got it.

A: Yes.

B: No.

Some disputes, though, are worked out privately, so to say, with one child doing both voices in presenting two sides in a dispute. One study of a 4-year-old noted that she would talk to herself for five to ten minutes at a time, doing two distinct voices as she worked on a conflict over some possession, showed concern with what was good versus bad, and often incorporated the voice of a peer as she worked on making sense of her social world. This work on one's social identity is also part of the path children follow as they become more aware of how to present themselves to others, and how to make use of language as they construct a social identity.

The dialogues externalized by this child involved assertions and denials, threats and insults, reconciliations and reciprocity. In these dialogues, each turn tended to be a move in an argument, with the different voices marked by pitch and voice quality. The arguments typically escalated, ending in moral judgements. They appear to reflect typical scripts for preschool interactions with peers, as in this dialogue (produced at age 4;3), where a bout of liking gives way to dislike and then turns back again:

> *Voice 1:* Do you like me?
> *Voice 2:* Yes.
> *Voice 1:* OK then I like you.
> *Voice 2:* Heh-heh. OK. Um, you know what I will do to you? Kill you.
> *Voice 1:* Well then, *I* don't like *you*.
> *Voice 2:* Then *I* don't like *you*. I will kill you.
> *Voice 1:* Ohhh. I like you.
> *Voice 2:* Then I like you. I won't kill you.

Other imaginary dialogues focus on reaching agreement in negotiation, on reciprocity of actions, on reconciliation. In some, the child sometimes uses the voices with third-person references as if two other people are talking about her, and then shifts back to presenting herself again in the first person, as *I*:

> *Voice A:* She doesn't know all those things. She doesn't know anything.
> *Voice B:* You're wrong. She doesn't know anything and *you* don't know anything.
> *Voice A/as self:* I know lots. I know *some* things. Mama knows lots of things. Papa doesn't know any.

Children also go over unresolved events where they have not succeeded, with one voice for the child and another for the critic-guide, as in the following imaginary dialogue:

> *Child/voice A:* Breaked.
> *Guide/voice B:* But, if you do it *slowly* [drawn out] it won't break, but *if you do it that way it will break.*
>
> *(continued)*

(continued)

Child/voice A:	I'mna do it slowly and it won't break. I'mna try. (sequence repeated several times, then): Did it fast, *then it breaked.* *Pretty* fast anyway. Did it *pretty fast.*
Guide/voice B:	Not at all fast. Not *at all* fast. Sorry, but not at all fast. Not at all, not at all fast. Sor-ry. *Not.*
Child/voice A:	I am really sorry, really, really sorry. But just can't.

These imaginary dialogues with peers seem to emerge as children realize they must learn how to deal with other children, at daycare and in kindergarten; they must work out how to collaborate and persuade, and how to negotiate, as they play and work together. They seem to play a role in children's construction of their own social identities, as viewed by others and by themselves, when they begin to have more intensive regular contact with peers.

The influence of peers also shows up in specific phonological and lexical features. After a year in preschool settings, for example, 4- and 5-year-olds converge in their language use. This convergence is independent of any influence from the teacher's speech or from the children's awareness of other local norms for language use. Effectively, the more children talk to each other, the more similar their speech becomes.

Telling stories

In their pretend-play, children often develop narratives about what Smurfs or action figures are doing, tell a story about the ongoing actions, and occasionally do the voice for one or other of the toys. In these early stories, they show they are talking in the story-world by using words that don't otherwise appear in their spontaneous speech, e.g. *meanwhile, instantly, once upon a time.* These are expressions that they hear in stories that are read to them, and which have thus been identified as appropriate for narrative.

Children's very earliest stories told without props (no pictures, no small toys) tend to be really minimal, on the order of one utterance and a coda: *The mouse runned upstairs. The end.* In one study of stories told by 3- to 5-year-olds in the course of conversation with their parents, the stories got longer with age (from an average length of 1.7 clauses to 2.8 clauses), and were told with an increasing number of turns. Most episodes in these stories were personal, based on events the children had recently participated in or observed. These stories, though, received only scant introductions, with occasional uses of *once* used on its own, and with endings marked simply by a change of topic. More striking though: these early stories made minimal use of the viewpoints present in the real versus the narrative world.

With a prop in the form of a wordless picture book, however, it is possible to track changes in how children tell the accompanying story, from age 3 up to 9, and compare their narratives to those of adults. This procedure makes it possible to compare storytelling skills across languages as well, both in terms of the overall story structure at a macro level, and in terms of the kinds of clauses and clause combinations children rely on at a micro level. Take micro-level differences with age. One critical element is how children use verbs as they recount events with a viewpoint and conceptual perspective appropriate for the episode being recounted.

As children look at picture books, for instance, they must segment the events shown into chunks they can describe. At age 3, children tend to treat each page as self-contained, and do little more than list the contents depicted. By age 5, they link a sequence of pictures, treating each one as an element in a larger episode in the story. Compare the first episode of *Frog, Where Are You?* (where a small boy's pet frog escapes from its jar and runs away) offered by a 3-year-old compared to a 5-year-old English speaker, each narrating the frog's escape while the boy is asleep:

> Child aged 3: *they're looking at it. and there's a frog. he's looking at the jar. cause his frog's not there* (whispering). *getting out.*
>
> Child aged 5: *well– there was a little boy. he liked– his pet frog and his pet dog– very much. he thinks they– they– he– the pets think– that– his– the little boy was proud of them. And then– he was sleeping– one night– and when he woke up– then– then– the frog– then the– then the frog– um got out of his bowl– and he went somewhere else–*

The 3-year-old jumps ahead to the picture where the boy and his dog look at the empty jar and back to the frog's climbing out, but the sequence of events is unclear. The 5-year-old offers a more coherent narrative. He distinguishes ongoing states (*sleeping*) from punctual events on the main story line (*woke up, got out, went*), introduces each character (*a little boy, his pet frog*), and then continues with definite references for the main character (*the little boy*) along with pronouns (*he*) for most of the later mentions.

As storytellers, children must choose an appropriate form for each verb so the storyteller presents a coherent account at each point in the narrative being presented. They can present an event as ongoing (*The bees were flying*) or completed (*The owl flew out*), for example, and a protagonist as an agent (*The boy looked for the frog*) or as the object affected (*The dog was caught*). Narrators track changes in location, with motion verbs and locative expressions; they make use of aspect on the verb (where this is available) to mark the start and end of an event; and they present changes of state, e.g. from *lost* to *found*, with choices of transitivity in the verb (transitive: *the boy lost his frog*, versus intransitive: *the frog ran away*) and voice (active: *the owl flew out*; passive: *the toy was hidden*). Children acquire all these devices eventually, but their skill in using them is limited to begin with. And, another factor in acquisition: the grammar of the language being acquired can lead to different characterizations of the same event across languages.

As children get older, they track characters across episodes, and introduce information about their current state of mind (e.g. *liked, was proud of*) to motivate actions and events. They distinguish background information (*while he was sleeping*) from foregrounded events (*the frog ran away*), and use past tense verbs to mark the events that form the main storyline. They also start to frame the whole story at the beginning, and then lead up to a climax and resolution. In doing this, they elaborate the telling at the clausal level, incorporating more of the devices available in the language as they gain more control of additional rhetorical options. And they add more planning at the macro level, visible in their overall framing for sequences of events in the narrative.

The options for doing all this differ from one language to another. Some languages have extensive marking on verbs to indicate the 'shape' of an event, with what is called *inceptive* aspect marking for the start of an event (e.g. *he began to run*), *durative* aspect for ongoing events that last (e.g. *he was running*), *iterative* aspect for repeated actions (e.g. *he tapped on the window*), and *completive* aspect for events that are now past (e.g. *the book fell on the floor*). Some languages rely on repetitions of a verb to mark duration (e.g. *it runs and runs and runs*); others have no aspect marking and rely on tense alone along with temporal expressions (*they began to run, they arrived later, he walked for an hour*, etc.).

Languages also differ in how they represent motion, manner, and direction in space, some combining motion and manner as in English and German (e.g. *stroll, meander, run, gallop*), others combine motion and direction as in French and Italian (e.g. French *entrer* 'go in', *monter* 'go up', *partir* 'go away'). Some languages rely on pronouns to track protagonists through each episode in a story; others lack pronouns and rely on the addressee's memory for information that is already in common ground in order to keep track of who is now being talked about.

In short, with age and experience, children become more advanced speakers who can refer flexibly as they choose their conceptual perspective for referring to specific entities and events, take different viewpoints, track particular characters over a series of episodes and actions, and so present a coherent story thread from beginning to end. Learning how to tell a good story takes years, and even 9-year-olds still have some way to go before they can tell stories really well.

Instructions and directions

Giving instructions also takes skill. At age 4, children offer simple instructions on how to play with a toy, or how to put a toy together to play with it. Here is 4-year-old JK's account of how to play with a garage with a dumping station and three trucks that carry marbles:

JK (to mother, explaining about dumping station): *you put it in here.*
<question from mother> *and then push it all the way in, and then you get marbles out here. you'll need gas. It* (= truck) *only has enough gas to go to the gas station. it backed in here. that's good.*
<question from Experimenter> *you have to make it go back up here. then you pick it* (= marble) *up and it goes back in.*

But when the same 4-year-old instructs Sara, aged 2, things sound different:

> *JK* (telling 2-year-old about dumping station): *I gave you it. you want to do something funny? put the marbles in here. put the marbles in here. I'll give you the marbles. now pour them in here. go up here. and pour them in here. now we have to dump it. dump it. no, not in here. pour it in here. pour it in here, okay? that's funny. no, not like that. I'll do it. see, Sara?*

Children aged 4 adapt their instructions to their addressees: they use longer utterances on average to adults, and shorter ones, with more repetitions, to 2-year-olds. They favour forms like *Hey* to adults to signal that what's coming up is of interest; with 2-year-olds, though, they use *Look*, *See*, and the child's name. They also use more imperatives to the younger children, telling them what to do, instead of describing what one *can* do with the toy.

Instructions for playing with a toy dumping station appear fairly straightforward compared to giving route directions for the path to trace on a town map. In one study of how well pairs of children could communicate using route directions, two children each had the identical, symmetrical map in front of them, and they each took turns to describe the path that the other child needed to follow with a small car through the town depicted on the map. The children could see each other (and each other's gestures), but, separated by a low barrier, they could not see the other's map or where the car actually was. Giving instructions for a specific route on the instruction-giver's map was challenging because the speaker had to keep in mind both his own viewpoint and that of the addressee, and then keep track of how to use terms like *right* and *left* as well as *in front of* and *behind*, together with descriptions of specific landmarks such as houses (distinguished by colour and number of windows) and bridges along the route to be traced.

Even 11-year-olds do not fare well in such tasks: they had particular trouble with *left* and *right*, in making clear whether they were taking their own viewpoint or their addressee's. They would also forget that there were two bridges, two green houses with two windows, and so on, and therefore fail to make their instructions clear enough. At the same time, their addressees often blithely assumed they had understood which path to follow, even when they hadn't. Keeping track, with language, of where to move a toy car on a town map presents children (and adults) with a remarkably difficult task. By age 14, children did better, both in making the relevant viewpoint clear in their instructions, and in following instructions from the other child. But adults did better still.

Summary

Perspective-taking operates at many levels, from very local (consider *dog* versus *pet*) in conversation up to rather complex in storytelling where the narrator must plan where to start and what perspective to present in each episode. Perspective is embodied in the language appropriate to particular social roles, when children enact being a small child, a father, a doctor, a teacher. There they must choose words and utterances appropriate to the relevant social role. Part of how they conceive of their own role as a child in a social setting such as kindergarten can sometimes be heard being worked out as in imaginary conversations. These require a slightly different idea of perspective, as children present two distinct voices in such exchanges, negotiating and debating different aspects of their emerging social identities.

In stories, the speaker's perspective can be discerned in the choices of words in referring expressions (compare *the kitten* versus *that animal*) and also of constructions that indicate whether the speaker is focussed on the object affected by an action, for instance, as in *The ball* rolled across the path, or on the agent who was the source of the relevant action, as in *The boy* rolled the ball across the path. Stories can be presented from just one viewpoint (that of just one character, usually the main actor), or they can follow several different viewpoints as the action shifts from one character to another. Perspectives, viewpoints, and voices all play a role as children acquire more adult-like skills in using language.

Chapter 9

More than one language at once

Many children are faced with learning not one but two or more languages from early on in childhood. For these children, part of what is involved is more complex because they have to track two systems at once as they are trying to break into language. They hear two distinct sound systems, and once they have started to sort out which sounds belong in each, along with which sequences of sounds form potential words, they need to map meanings to word forms, just as they would in acquiring a single language. They must also work out which words correspond (more or less) across the two languages they are exposed to. And as they start combining words to produce longer utterances, they must also attend to where there is (and isn't) equivalence across constructions too.

Two systems from the start

Children exposed to two languages, from birth or from some point in their first few years, are exposed to two sound systems. These may be fairly close in many respects, as in the case of Dutch, English, and German, or they may quite distinct as in French versus English or Japanese. For each language, children need to distinguish possible sounds and sequences of sounds, so they can use the sound patterns characteristic of each language not only to identify possible words, but also to distinguish the two languages. They are often helped in this respect by differences in the patterns found in words (consider stress-timing in English, with one primary stressed syllable per word, versus syllable-timing in French, with equal stress on each syllable in a word), and by differences in the intonation contours speakers use.

Early on in acquisition, children acquiring two languages appear to go through stages in production similar to those observed in monolingual children. Their early attempts at words tend to be single syllables constructed from a consonant and vowel, and these generally bear little resemblance to the intended targets. At this early a stage too, it is often difficult to tell which language the child is attempting. It is not until children can approximate adult words rather better in production that it is generally clear what their target is, and hence from which language.

Two vocabularies: early doublets

One measure of how children are managing as they acquire two languages has been to look at which doublets they know – which equivalents or near-equivalents in the two languages. For example, a 1-year-old might begin with a few terms from English and a few from French, none of which overlap in meaning. But once they have accumulated around fifty words, children add more and more doublets, sometimes soliciting them directly from the adult. In effect, as soon as children become aware that they are dealing with two systems, with contrast applying only within each language, they should start adding doublets, and they do. Take Caitlin, who was acquiring Dutch and English from birth. By age 2, she produced some 373 terms in Dutch and 388 in English. And 299 of these were doublets. She had English equivalents for 80 per cent of her Dutch words, and Dutch equivalents of 77 per cent of her English words. These proportions at around age 2 are typical.

As children learn more about each language, though, the status of many earlier doublets becomes more complicated: relatively few words in a domain have fully equivalent translations into another language. One part of the relevant domain may be divided between two terms in one language but need only one term in the other. Consider the relations between the French and Dutch terms for 'bottle' and 'grape' or 'raisin', compared to the apparently more straightforward equivalents for 'dish', 'plate', and 'bowl' (though these too are actually more complex than the listing below suggests):

French	Gloss	Dutch	Gloss
biberon	baby's bottle	**fles**	bottle
bouteille	bottle		
raisin	grape, raisin	**druif**	grape
		rozijn	raisin
plat	dish, plate	**schaal**	dish
assiette	plate	**bord**	plate
bol	bowl	**kom**	bowl

In short, children have to work out, for each language, as they acquire more and more words, how each semantic domain is structured. Does it contain different words for different kinds of bottle, or for different kinds of chair, as in French (*chaise, fauteuil*), or different words for different states of a grape, as in Dutch *druif* versus *rozijn*? Children must build up a vocabulary for each language they are acquiring, and, in doing so, attend to how the words are used by the (adult) speakers around them. While there has been little research on how children build up semantic domains in two languages at once, provided they are supplied with similar information about new words and how these are related to words they already know in the relevant language, they should follow much the same path as children exposed to just one language. Indeed, as they learn about superordinate terms in a domain, they are also prompted for doublets, as in this exchange between Anouk, a bilingual child acquiring French and Dutch, and her French-speaking mother:

Mother: ça c'est un fruit.   'that, that's a fruit'
Anouk (2;3.13): ***aabei***.   'strawberry' (in Dutch)
Mother: **aabei**, comment tu dis en   'strawberry, what do you
   français?   say in French?'

> *Anouk:* (no response)
> *Mother:* Non, comment tu dis en   'No, how do you say
>   français **aardbeien**?   *strawberries* in French?
>   Comment je dis moi?   What do I say?'
>
> *Anouk: faise.*   'strawberry' (in French)
> *Mother:* fraise oui.   'strawberry yes'

Notice too that the mother offers the conventional forms of the two words, in the Dutch plural *aardbeien* (compared to the child's attempt, **aabei**) and in the French *fraise* (following the child's version, *faise*), and so also offers feedback on how the words are said, in both languages.

Vocabulary size

Researchers have established fairly extensive norms for vocabulary sizes during the first two years of talking, using a questionnaire called the MacArthur Communicative Development Inventory, or CDI for short. This allows for early assessment of which words young children understand and which they produce, with parents checking off all the applicable terms. One question is whether children exposed to two languages from the start learn the same overall number of words as monolinguals, but split them between the two languages. In other words, such children would produce only half as many words in each of their languages as the corresponding monolingual children would. However, a comparison of Dutch/French bilinguals with monolingual Dutch-learning children shows that bilingual children are in fact in the same range for production vocabulary as monolinguals: compare the ranges for monolingual Dutch with the range for Dutch only in bilinguals, and the range for both languages combined in the bilingual sample.

Vocabulary range in production	13 months	20 months
Monolingual Dutch	1–71	19–531
Bilinguals: Dutch only	0–68	4–642
Bilinguals: Dutch + French	0–82	14–1234

As children get older, of course, their vocabulary for each language may be extended in different ways, in different domains. For example, for children learning both French and English, if the school language is French, they will learn to talk about historical events, geographical features, mathematical operations, and biological phenomena in French, but have a rather sketchier grasp of how to talk about these areas in English. This is true of any speakers making use of more than one language: activities often call on one language more than the other, and language use for particular activities tends to become specialized by language. The language chosen for use will differ for home versus work, just as for activities like sailing versus gardening, or birdwatching versus skating.

Early word-combinations and language mixing

Bilingual children produce most of their early word-combinations within a single language, and with functions similar to those found in the early word-combinations of children acquiring just one language. They use them to comment on activities, identify possessors, point out features or properties of objects, to make requests and to reject them. These first word-combinations emerge during the same time frame as for monolingual children, starting at some point between 1;3 and 1;11, and they appear in both languages, as in the examples from Manuela with two-word combinations in both Spanish and English. How extensive their first word-combinations are in each language, of course, depends on the size of their vocabulary. The point to note here is that the majority of their early word-combinations generally draw on just one language at a time.

Portuguese

(a) Karin (1;10): *mama peix.*	'mummy (is drawing a) fish'
(b) *Mikael* (1;5): *roupa papa.*	'clothes papa' (as laundry was sorted)
(c) *Mikael* (1;10): *cabelo amarelo.*	'hair yellow' (discussing hair colours in family photos)

Spanish		
(d) *Manuela* (1;7): *no cama.*	'no bed' (not wanting to go to bed)	
English		
(e) *Manuela* (1;7): *mummy off.*	(wanting her mother to take the mother's coat off)	

Although children learning more than one language start to combine words within the same age range as children exposed to just one language, they occasionally combine words from the two languages. This may be because they don't know the relevant word and so 'borrow' from their other language, or because they can retrieve the relevant word from one language faster than from the other. (Sometimes a word in one language may be easier to say, as when an English-Spanish 1-year-old never attempted English *milk* with its final /–lk/ cluster of consonants – saying *bottle* instead – but willingly produced *leche* in Spanish.)

Mixing in early word-combinations: Norwegian and English

Tomas (2;0):	**der va** *hens*	'there were hens'
Tomas (2;3):	**jeg har masse** *toys*	'I have lots of toys'
	og jeg er *boy*	'and I am (a) boy'
Siri (2;1):	**må** *leave*	'must leave'
Siri (2;2):	**mer** *paper*	'more paper'
	mer *milk*	'more milk'
	have **mer**	'have more'
	jeg *down*	'I down'
Siri (2;5):	**den** *cast on*	'that cast on'
	nei kan *do it*	'no I can do it'
	kan *do it* **jeg**	'can do it I'
Siri (2;7):	**jeg kan ikke** *do that*	'I can not do that'

Language mixing, both in early word-combinations and later on, to some extent seems to involve function words or grammatical morphemes from one language combined with nouns and verbs from the other language. One child acquiring Norwegian and English, for example, produced a number of early word-combinations of this type at 2;1 and 2;2, when she relied on pronouns (*jeg* = I), negatives (*ikke* = not), modal verbs (*ma* = must; *kan* = can), and quantifiers (*mer* = more) from Norwegian combined with nouns and verbs from English.

Similar kinds of mixing have been reported for other young children acquiring two languages at once, with the children tending to draw on pronouns and other grammatical elements from one language and content words (mainly nouns and verbs) from the other:

More language mixing in early word-combinations

French/English –	*Tiffany* (2;5): **I wan** pas **chair**	'I don't want (a) chair'
	Gene (2;7): **I** *pousse là*	'I push there'
	Gene (3;1): **I** *peux pas* **wash the** *cou* **me**!	'I can't wash my neck'
	Will (3;3): *moi* **do this** *moi.*	'Me do this, me'
French/German –	*Iv* (2;8): **du, du** *aimes ça la soupe?*	'you, you like that the soup?'
	A (3;3): *Sonja a – je* **schenk** *ça*	'Sonja has – I give this'
German/Italian –	*Lisa* (2;10): *jetzt* **faccio** *ein fisch*	'now I'm doing a fish'
	Lisa (3;9): *Lisa hat* ge**balla**	'Lisa has danced'

These early instances of mixing bear some resemblance to the kinds of code switching often found in the speech of bilingual adults, where speakers readily switch from one language to another as they are talking, often in mid-utterance. But code switching seems to be facilitated by the speakers' familiarity with the different language communities and by their desire, for instance, to use the original names for films, book characters, and other phenomena popularized in one culture first and then spread to others. Code switching, then, can indicate cultural ease and/or expertise on the speaker's part. It is common is most bilingual communities. When it comes to children, they tend to follow the adult's lead, with the amount of switching they do generally matched to the amount used by their interlocutor. If the child's father does less of this than the child's mother, for example, the child's speech will differ on this dimension, depending on which parent is the interlocutor.

Language choice and addressee

Children appear to be quite adept at choosing the 'right' language for the addressee from early on. In part, this is mostly likely driven by adult speakers' choices of language and what each adult generally uses in talking with the child, hence part of their common ground. When addressed by unfamiliar adults, of course, children can also depend on linguistic clues to the language they should use on that occasion – clues from the sound system and the vocabulary that they hear from them. Even 1- and 2-year-olds, though, are consistently at or over 85 per cent, and often well over 90 per cent, in their choices of the appropriate language for their interlocutors. This, of course, is where doublets play an important role. Having the words available makes it easier to choose the right language and still be able to communicate one's interests and desires at an early age.

The sensitivity bilingual children display to language choices for the addressee is also attested in their repairs to language choice. When addressees give signs of not understanding, children as young as 2 will switch to their other language. They also switch when asked by a parent, and are often presented with their mother or father asking the child to 'say it the way I say it' (i.e. in the appropriate language). As children get older, they also often spontaneously repeat what they were saying in the other language when an interlocutor gives signs of incomprehension, as when Nic (3;4) followed up his use of the English word *boat* in *N'est pas une boat* ('is not a **boat**), in response to the adult's *Quoi?* ('what'), by saying *Euh, c'est un bateau bateau* ('uh, it's a boat boat').

Percentage of utterances produced in the right language for the addressee		
(a) English/Latvian	– Maija (1;3)	93%
	– (1;9)	85%
	– (2;2)	96%
(b) German/Italian	– Lukas (1;8)	90%
(c) English/German	– Sofia (1;11.23)	95%
	– (2;4-2;6)	97%
	– (2;7-2;9)	96%
(d) Dutch/French	– Anouk (2;6)	88%

Notice that choosing the right language for an addressee in the family offers further evidence that children keep track of what their addressees do (and don't) know. In this case, children must depend on common ground already established with each addressee in choosing the language to use. And they sometimes express surprise when they hear someone who generally speaks French, say, speaking in Dutch to a visitor. This too suggests that children associate each language with specific people, and expect to hear and use a particular language with each person they know.

Adding complexity

As children's utterances become longer, they also become more complex, combining more small grammatical elements with nouns and verbs, and so making children's intentions clearer when they speak. Here too, as children attempt more complex utterances, they may draw on the grammatical elements – articles, prepositions, negatives, and so on – from one language, usually their dominant language, and combine them with nouns and verbs from the weaker language. This is sometimes characterized as interference, but it could equally be conceived of as a form of compensation where the children don't yet have as good a grasp of the grammatical elements in the weaker of their two languages, and so rely on elements that are already well established.

This can be seen in the mixed utterances from two sisters, both dominant in French for production but with consistent exposure to English from their mother, after a two-month stay in the US, where for the first time they heard and had to interact with a wide variety of English speakers. They were recorded at regular intervals during this stay. Towards the end of the stay, the younger child, Tiffany, at 2;5, produced mixed utterances 24 per cent of the time (113 of 471 utterances), and 80 per cent of these mixed utterances contained grammatical elements drawn from French. Her older sister, Odessa, 3;8, also produced mixed utterances, but did so only 11 per cent of the time (in 39 of 360 utterances), and 92 per cent of these mixed utterances contained grammatical elements drawn from French.

Mixing in more elaborate utterances: French/English

Tiffany (2;5):	*coffee **à** mommy*	'mommy's coffee'
	*see **le** kitty*	'see the kitty'
	***pas** mommy that shoe*	'that's not mommy's shoe'
	***ça** mommy coffee*	'that mommy's coffee'
	***c'est** cold*	'it's cold'
Odessa (3;8):	*what this **tu** got?*	'what(s) this you got'
	*the sun is coming **dans** my eyes*	'the sun is getting in my eyes'
	*a daddy **avec** a child on his shoulders*	'a daddy with a child on his shoulders'
	*take **la** spoon*	'take the spoon'
	***tu** do what **avec le** table?*	'you do what with the table?'
	***mais** I want Aunt Hannah not coming*	'but I don't want Aunt Hannah to come'

Other researchers have reported similar patterns in mixed utterances, with reliance on grammatical elements, and also word order, from the dominant language. Consider the placement of *not* in Odessa's last utterance, and these examples from Mario, who was acquiring Spanish and English, as well as from another child acquiring English and

German who made certain word-order errors in German more consistent with his other language, English.

Some more mixed utterances

Mario (3;3):	*mufete*	'Eng. *move* + Sp. –e + Sp. reflexive *te* = move!'
	I'm **sak**ing	'Sp. *sacar* "take out" = I'm taking (it) out'
	I no have hungwy	'Sp. *no tengo hambre* = I'm not hungry'
	Let's go play in da floor	'Sp. *en* = "in ~ on" = on the floor'
	I have too manys cars	'Sp. plural agreement with *cars* on *many*'

Some word order issues for a child acquiring English and German

Child (2;7) *Hund <u>nicht kommt</u> rein* (for G. kommt nicht rein = 'dog doesn't come here')

Child (3;2) *Ich möchte <u>tragen dich</u>* (for G. dich tragen = 'I want to carry you')

Child (3;8) *Ich <u>sitzen noch hier</u>* (for G. Ich sitze hier noch = 'I'm still sitting here')

While mixing patterns like these shows that children will draw on their dominant language as they start to use the non-dominant language more, there is little research on when children start to use more complex utterances, for example, adding relative clauses to modify information in a referring expression, or talking about sequences of events. But children start to tell stories, whether imaginary narratives or retellings of what is happening in a series of pictures, from at least age 4. But just as with monolingual children, they take time to master the linguistic options that are useful in storytelling: pronouns for the main character, keeping track of the sequence of events, linking background information to foregrounded actions, and so on. Exposure to the options favoured in any one language is critical as children learn to do more complicated things with each of their languages.

Bilingualism, multilingualism

From a social point of view, being bilingual has a number of advantages. First of all, much of the world is bilingual or multilingual, so learning more than one language early on offers more options for cross-cultural communication. In particular, knowing two languages allows for roots in two (or more) communities. This is a vital element in maintaining links between different generations, something that is particularly important among immigrant groups, with parents or grandparents who may not have acquired the language of the country where they have settled. Learning two or more languages early on allows speakers to maintain their connections to different cultures.

What is important here is to realize that being bilingual does not require that speakers have fully equivalent skills in two distinct languages, but rather that they are skilled native speakers who use both languages in specialized ways. This may mean one language for school, and another for home; one language for family and local friends, the other for people at work; or one language for use locally, at home and at work, and the other used for more distant aspects of work, away from the local area. Actual patterns of language use vary with the community and with the number of languages in common use.

Summary

Children acquiring more than one language at once set up two systems from the start. They distinguish the sounds and sounds patterns of their languages. They start to acquire doublets in their vocabulary, being offered and asking for equivalent terms in each language. And they go through similar stages, at similar ages, to those observed in children acquiring just one language alone. As they get older, they may favour one language in production, making it their dominant language, and rely on that source at first to supply grammatical elements like articles, prepositions, and even word endings (e.g. English *–ing* on verbs for 'ongoing action' or Hebrew *–im* on nouns for 'more than one') in their other language.

Just as for children learning a single language, they depend on exposure, practice, and feedback. The more exposure they get to each language, the more their development resembles what goes on in monolingual development for that language. But children who are learning more than one language at once do so in a variety of contexts, with parents who speak a variety of languages: some hear one language from one parent, the other only from the other. But parents have to choose which language to speak to each other, and that may tip the balance in the end towards more exposure to one of the languages being acquired. The home language may be different from the community language, so school may tip the balance away from the home language, and so on. All of these factors need to be taken into account in assessing how similar, and how different, the setting is for acquiring one versus more than one language at a time.

Chapter 10

Process in acquisition

How do children learn the *forms* of language – the sounds, words, inflections, word structure, lexical organization, and syntactic constructions – and how to use those forms? How do children connect forms and meanings? That is, how do children do the mapping from form to meaning? What is the basis for an initial meaning assignment? What resources do they draw on as they set up meanings for forms in memory? How much of the conventional meaning do they take in on their first exposure to a new word? How do children add to the initial meaning they have assigned to a word form? These questions about mapping stand at the heart of the process of acquisition. Children have to solve the form/meaning link before they can begin to do anything with language.

What happens when a 1-year-old hears the adult say 'Look at the bunny' while watching a pet rabbit eating lettuce? The child is already attending to the rabbit, and the adult is emphasizing that attention with *Look*. Then the adult labels the object in the focus of their joint attention, using a referring expression: *the bunny*. The mapping here, based on joint attention, would be whatever the child has taken in about the rabbit as a whole on this occasion – animal-shaped, furry, long ears, four-legged, eyes on the side of the head, and so on. Later on, he might add to such features some information about characteristic movement, possible range of colours, foodstuffs, general size of rabbits, and so on. This information must be stored in memory, linked to *bunny* (and later to *rabbit* too), so that the child can use the mapping currently stored to interpret subsequent uses of the word from other speakers.

To understand what a speaker is saying, children need to take in the stream of sounds from that speaker, segment it into any recognizable words, and 'look up' those words in memory. This allows them to arrive at some meaning for that utterance given that combination of words, word order, and intonation contour (identified as signalling a question or an assertion, say), as well as the physical context of the adult utterance. Was the utterance produced as part of a conversation? In response to a topic already in play? Did it initiate a new topic? Did it require a response from the child?

Consider the adult who asks a 1;6-year-old the question: 'Where are your sandals?' This child is familiar with the word *sandal*, and has previously demonstrated understanding of it. The initial word in the adult utterance, *where*, is also familiar as a cue to find something. On hearing these two words, then, the child looks around for his sandals. He draws on his memory of the form/meaning link for *sandal* and the cue to look for something, the adult's use of *where*. To answer the question, the child must identify the location of the sandals, by pointing, by pointing and saying *there*, or by identifying their location verbally, e.g. *in the box*. Planning an answer therefore involves the following steps:

(a) Start with an idea of the answer.
(b) Retrieve any relevant words from memory.
(c) Place nouns and verbs into the appropriate slots in the construction chosen.
(d) Add inflections and grammatical morphemes as needed to the nouns and verbs.
(e) Execute the utterance, with appropriate timing, as soon as possible, in the next turn.

To answer a question children must first understand it. Indeed, they must rely on various skills in both comprehension and production as they amass more information about the forms and meanings of the language. They have to develop a set of skills that enable them to analyse the speech stream, track recurring sequences or chunks that have become familiar and to which they have assigned some meaning, check on their own productions, and make repairs as needed.

Processes in acquisition

What processes underlie the development of each of these skills? First of all, children must be able to **analyse** the speech stream into familiar chunks to which they have already attached some meaning. To do this, they need to be familiar with the sounds of the language, and to recognize sequences of sounds they have heard before – often a word but sometimes more than a word. (The ability to break up the speech stream into shorter familiar sequences of sounds appears to be well established by 7–8 months when infants can differentiate familiar from unfamiliar subsequences prior to any mapping of meanings to forms.) As they acquire more words, their ability to analyse the speech stream allows them to identify more and more linguistic elements.

Second, they need to **track** the occurrences of each element they recognize in the speech they hear. They do that to strengthen memory traces for specific words and other linguistic units. This enables children to track unfamiliar sequences as they recur, whether these are words or phrases, and to add analysis of how they are being used, together with any information about recurring contexts. Effectively, children appear to track frequency of occurrence, something that adult speakers remain sensitive to. Adult judgements of frequency, in fact, have been used to assess 'age of acquisition' for different words in the lexicon and to track age-of-acquisition norms in different populations.

Third, they must **monitor** how they themselves produce an utterance. When speakers talk, they monitor their speech to make sure they have produced what they intended to say. And when their production goes wrong, they generally correct it immediately themselves. Even very young children monitor their utterances, trying to 'fix' the pronunciation of a word to make it more recognizable. But what is their basis for deciding there is something wrong with the utterance produced? Speakers appear to use whatever representations they have stored in memory as templates for what their words should sound like. These representations allow them to recognize words heard from others and they also provide templates for producing words themselves.

These matter because, if they are to make themselves understood, children must produce words that are recognizable.

Fourth, to achieve this, they must deal with any mismatches between the template of a word in memory and their own production of that word. When they detect a mismatch, they need to **repair** their own speech to match the template form they have stored in memory. Making repairs to their own speech is not easy for young children: they often lack the necessary articulatory skill, as in Brenda's attempts at the word *fan* (see Chapter 7), and they also may have to work hard to get rid of entrenched pronunciations for particular word forms such as over-regularized noun plurals like *mouses* – a mismatch to conventional *mice*, or past tense verb forms like *comed, see-d, buyed*, or *sitted* – mismatches to conventional *came, saw, bought*, and *sat* (see Chapter 5). Self-initiated repairs are common, even in very young children's speech, but children also respond early on to other-initiated repairs from their adult interlocutors of the form: 'What?', 'What did you say?', 'Umh?' or 'Eh?', 'What was that?', or echoic questions that repeat part of the child's utterance, as in 'You're going where?', 'You saw what?'

Children's ability to monitor and repair their own speech is critical for effecting **change** in their language. The forms they store in memory are based on their perception of the adult forms they hear in interaction. In monitoring their own speech, they compare their own productions to the forms heard from adults, and stored in memory. When they detect a mismatch, they try to change their own version to achieve a better match. This impulse to match the conventional forms in the speech community ultimately allows children to be understood more accurately and more swiftly, and so streamlines their ability to communicate using language. Notice that by matching the adult forms produced in the speech community, children gradually change their own language to something closer, if not identical, to the adult language spoken around them.

Errors of omission and commission

In making changes, children must deal with two major types of mismatches. First, many mismatches involve **omissions**, errors of omission, where children have left out elements that are obligatory in adult speech, as in *two bird* for 'two birds' or *Me put shoe* for 'I put the shoes there'. Common omissions include definite and indefinite articles, pronouns, inflectional endings on verbs and nouns, and prepositions; auxiliary and modal verbs, question words, and conjunctions. Managing to add in just the right piece of missing material takes attention and time. Errors of omission are very common early on.

Second, children must deal with errors of **commission**. This happens, for example, when they choose the wrong word and adults follow up with the right one (e.g. the adult's offer of the noun *eel* for the child's erroneous proposal of *snake*, or the adult's transitive verb *drop* after an erroneous child transitive use of intransitive *fall*); when children produce an over-regularized plural noun (e.g. *mans*, *foots*, *sheeps*) and, in the next turn, hear adults use the conventional version, namely *men, feet, sheep*; or when they produce an over-regularized verb (e.g. *breaked, bringed, digged*) in place of adult *broke, brought*, and *dug*. These errors become commoner as children learn more of the language.

Mismatches provide an important source of information for change, and children are sensitive, from early on, to how things are said and how adults use language around them. Using the language in the same way as others marks them as members of the community. Adherence to community norms appears characteristic of conventional systems such as language. And it is essential for the learning of any conventional system. It shows up later in schoolchildren who wish to show that they belong to a particular sub-community within the school. The same applies to adults who use in-group talk and terminology to show membership in a sub-community, whether they are sailors, tennis players, birdwatchers, doctors, or teachers. Language connects people socially, indicating their community memberships.

Mismatches also provide an incentive for change when children suffer from failures of communication or experience active miscommunication. The adult may be unable to understand anything (as in some conversations with 1-year-old Brenda), or may misunderstand a particular utterance. To rectify a misunderstanding, the child often has to change the forms produced in the original utterance. In short, children can make use of their monitor-and-repair system to change their own language. Change is integral to the process of acquisition – a process that takes place in bits and pieces, in fits and starts, with the occasional interim generalization, and with the gradual recognition of related forms and the construction of paradigms, as children slowly put together all the elements of the language they are acquiring.

What do children need to acquire a first language?

How are these mechanisms used in the process of acquisition? There are at least three factors required. First, **exposure**: children need to hear the target language in a range of contexts and activities as adults talk with their children, as they propose topics and take up topics proffered by children, and follow them up in conversation. This both exposes children to the language and allows them to observe adult usage. Second, when children make errors of omission or commission, they benefit from immediate **feedback** from their interlocutors, feedback offered in the next turn as adults accept or check up on what they mean. When this feedback consists of a reformulation containing a conventional way to say what the child seemed to intend, children can make an instant, on-the-spot comparison between their own erroneous utterance and the adult version, and then (eventually) opt for the adult version.

D (2;4.29, being carried): *don't fall me downstairs!*
Father: Oh, I wouldn't **drop** you downstairs.

Third, children need to **practise** what they know, and the more practice they get the better. Exposure, feedback, and practice together underpin the process of acquisition. As they practise, children focus on expressing their intentions with the appropriate speech acts and content, given what they wish to express. They choose the words that present a particular perspective. They greet, describe activities, make requests; they give instructions; they play at make-believe with parents and caregivers, peers and siblings; they tell stories. And they work on using language to construct their own social identity. In all this, they register the kind of speech people use in different roles, and how gender and status affect linguistic choices. They will also learn to tell jokes, make puns, and coin new words as needed, among the myriad things speakers do with language every day.

Learning a first language or a second: what's the difference?

Can the study of first-language acquisition throw light on learning a second language later in life? In some respects, yes. Let's begin with some basic comparisons: if we count up the hours spent in verbal interaction and hence working on a first language from age 1 to age 4, estimated at ten hours a day, we get the following:

Acquiring a first language

10 hours a day × 7 days = 70 hours a week
70 hours a week × 52 weeks = 3640 hours in a year
From age 1;0 to age 4;0, this amounts to **10,920** hours

How does this 10,000 hours and more compare to learning a second language at age 20? Notice that the setting is very different: (a) 20-year-olds are already highly competent in one language; (b) they get little exposure to the second language outside the classroom; (c) they have few opportunities to practise; (d) they have to deal with pragmatic restrictions on getting feedback from more expert speakers. All told, learners of a second language typically spend less than 5 per cent of the time that first-language learners spend on learning from age 1 to age 4.

Acquiring a second (or a third) language as an adult

1 hour a day in class,
plus 1 hour for language lab visits = 6 hours a week
6 hours a week for 30 weeks = 180 hours (in the academic year)
In 3 years of classes = **540 hours**

There are other differences between acquiring a first language and acquiring a second, third, or fourth language in adulthood. To begin with, a first language offers extensive exposure to the target language on a daily basis in conversation, but for adult learners of a second language, there is much less general exposure, and learners typically hear very little of the language on a daily basis in the early stages. Second, there are many fewer opportunities for practice with others, either in understanding or in speaking. Third, first-language acquisition offers many occasions for feedback from more expert speakers, occasions that young children attend to, and make use of. But with a later-acquired second language, such feedback is virtually absent, for two reasons. First, each teacher generally has from fifteen to as many as thirty students in a class and can attend to only one spoken error at a time. In fact, errors may simply be collected and listed at the end of class, so the feedback may often occur long past the point when each particular error was made. But correction in feedback is optimal when it is immediate. Second, adult speakers may fear losing face when offered corrective feedback in conversation, and this tends to constrain native speakers so they generally avoid offering corrections as long as they think they have understood what the second-language speaker intended. Even when they are asked to provide feedback on errors, many native speakers are reluctant to offer it to adult learners.

Finally, adult second-language learners already know a language well, so they have some idea of the kinds of information they might wish to convey: what is hard is to learn a new set of conventions for doing this. The basic setting for second-language acquisition is therefore radically different from that found in first-language acquisition.

Interestingly, the number of hours that children spend from age 1 to age 4 easily amounts to the 10,000 hours that have been proposed as a baseline for any form of expertise, whether in gymnastics, violin playing, or chess. Acquisition of a first language could in fact be viewed as a form of expertise, with a variety of usage skills applied in language comprehension and in language production. Moreover, children continue to hear (and read) more and more complex language as they get older still; they practise using this language on a daily basis, and they continue to get feedback in various forms on errors, all beyond the age of 4.

More than one language at once

Take another common setting for acquisition: what happens when children acquire two languages at once, either with exposure to both from birth, or else with exposure to the second within their first few years? In general, the patterns of acquisition in both languages resemble those of a single first language. But there are some differences. When children hear one language from one parent, and another from the other, they may end up hearing less of each language than they might have had with both parents using a single language. Yet careful comparison of monolingual and bilingual children shows little disadvantage in the bilinguals. At 13 months, bilingual children exposed to both Dutch and French may even understand more Dutch words than monolinguals. At 20 months, monolingual Dutch children may manage more words (comprehension and production combined) than bilinguals. But researchers have found no group differences for comprehension or production in Dutch. The general stages children go through also appear to be the same as they start to combine words, for example, and add inflections and grammatical morphemes. They acquire native phonology in their production of words in both languages, as well as native mastery of morphology and syntax.

The social setting for bilingualism is important. Bilinguals rarely learn to use both languages equally in every setting they encounter: they typically use one language in one set of contexts and the other elsewhere (e.g. as adults – at home versus at work). Their choice of language may also depend on the person or group they are interacting with. So speakers' uses become specialized in slightly different ways, even when they display considerable or complete overlap in many core uses of each language. Unless children are growing up in a bilingual community, there also comes a point when they get more exposure to one language than the other. For instance, when they start school, they realize that most people in the community speak only one of the two languages they have been acquiring. Children react to this differently: some opt to speak only the majority language but retain good comprehension of the other language spoken at home. Others adopt one language for home and one for school. Others distinguish all their addressees according to language choice and use. Parents can set some of the agenda here, but this doesn't always work out predictably. To maintain both languages, children need exposure, practice, and feedback with both, with as many different speakers as possible, for as long as possible.

Disorders and language development

Some researchers have assumed that we can identify specific brain areas, even specific genes, which affect the course of language acquisition. They have argued that by looking at language-disordered populations, we can find out about specific linguistic areas in the brain and what is essential to their development. Language disorders display different defects: children on the high-functioning end of the autism spectrum, for example, display a signal lack of social and pragmatic skills. Children with Williams syndrome appear superficially to have good linguistic skills even with very low intelligence, but closer inspection suggests that they too fail to observe many social cues in conversation. Children with Specific Language Impairment (SLI) are delayed overall in their acquisition of language, but not all in the same way. All these disorders present delays and imperfect acquisition of various kinds.

Can we make inferences from language disorders as to what is essential to the normal process of acquisition? The issue here is that general development in these children is affected from the very start by the deficit they suffer from. So their developmental course, all along, is different from the course followed by normally developing children. Until we know much more about brain development and genetic development on the one hand, and on the other about children's patterns of non-normal language development and, for example, any compensatory strategies they rely on (if they do, that is), we can't assume that language disorders will cast any light on the process of normal language development. Although some researchers have taken this position, innatists have argued that no genetic variation per se could affect the acquisition of specific paradigms in a language, such as the inflection of irregular verbs, the development of particular areas of vocabulary, or the late development (even the non-development) of certain pragmatic skills. Yet children with specific language disorders typically display just these problems in development from early on.

To discover the full story here, we will need at least three things: (a) a detailed account of how nature (here, genes and neurological development) interacts with nurture (the actual language use such children are exposed to and any feedback they get); (b) a full account of how different areas of language – phonology, morphology, lexicon, syntax, and pragmatics – work together in normal development, and (c) an account of the developmental course children follow for each subsystem in their first language, in the normal case compared to the non-normal one. At the moment, we lack the full story here on all three dimensions.

Language universals

Languages have evolved in certain ways that seem to make language-processing, whether in comprehension or production, easier for their users. For example, languages tend to exhibit certain regularities in word order, with many nearly always adhering to a Subject-Verb-Object order as in English, e.g. *He will hit the ball*, while others observe a Subject-Object-Verb order as in Dutch, e.g. *ik wil je helpen* 'I want you to-help = I want to help you'. These two, SVO and SOV, are the dominant orders found across languages. The Subject, usually an animate agent, is generally placed first in both orders. The consistency here, researchers have argued, allows speakers to assign a preliminary meaning upon hearing a novel utterance, and even if the Subject term is an unfamiliar proper name or an unfamiliar noun, say, children, like adults, can still assume that this word is likely to refer to an animate agent. And when speakers of such languages diverge from the usual word order, they typically mark this with stress on the word or phrase that is out of place, or with a special intonation contour.

Basic word orders are associated with consistencies in order in other constructions in the relevant languages. Compare some of the patterns found in VO languages versus OV languages:

VO languages (35%)	OV languages (44%)
Verb + Object	Object + Verb
Auxiliary + Main Verb	Main Verb + Auxiliary
Preposition + Noun	Noun + Postposition
Noun + Relative Clause	Relative Clause + Noun
Noun + Possessive	Possessive + Noun
Noun + Adjective	Adjective + Noun
Noun + Demonstrative	Demonstrative + Noun
Noun + Number	Number + Noun

Consistencies like these should make it easier for speakers to keep track of which linguistic elements 'go together' as they process what they hear and plan what to say. Agreement plays a similar role, as when an adjective agrees in gender and number with its noun (e.g. *le ballon vert* 'the-masc ball-masc green-masc = the green ball', compared to *la maison verte* 'the-fem house-fem green-fem = the green house'). In the same way, verbs agree with their subjects in number and person (and sometimes gender), e.g. *le garçon il viendra en retard* 'the-masculine-singular boy-masculine-singular he-masculine-singular come-future-3person-singular late = the boy will come late'. Some languages show agreement in case marking as well as in gender, number, and person, and so offer still more information about how to group the words uttered for interpretation or production.

How soon do children attend to and make use of word order? The evidence is unclear. They make rather inconsistent use of word order in their earliest word-combinations, and appear to use it to mark given followed by new information, rather than to mark grammatical relations. But as they get older, they observe word order in adjective-and-noun as well as noun-and-relative-clause combinations in word-order languages. The basic ordering of S with VO or OV is generally well established in 4- and 5-year-olds' utterances, as is that of possessive to object-possessed, noun and demonstrative, and noun and number.

In the lexical domain, all languages have expressions for spatial dimensions like height, width, and distance. In English, these dimensions are described with such adjective pairs as *high* and *low*, *wide* and *narrow*, *far* and *near*. The first adjective in such pairs describes extent along the dimension, the second lack of extent relative to some standard. The terms for extent appear in neutral questions (*How high is that hill?*) and in measure phrases (*That ladder is 2 metres high*), while those for lack of extent are sometimes expressed by the equivalent of a negative prefix like *un-* combined with the positive adjective, e.g. *un-deep* or *non-far*.

Again, these general patterns for encoding dimensions in space show up in the course of acquisition. Children learn some spatial adjective pairs early, with *big* and *small* leading the pack in English. In general, they master positive adjectives that encode extent before their negative counterparts. They also master adjectives with simpler meanings before those that are more complex, more specific in meaning. For example, they typically acquire both *big* and *small* (general size) before they take on *high* and *low* (vertical extent) or *long* and *short* (horizontal extent). Terms for dimensions like height and length are acquired before children master terms for secondary dimensions like width and depth: *wide* (secondary, non-vertical) and *deep* (secondary or tertiary, non-vertical), as in *The table was 3 metres long and 1 metre wide*, or *The pool was 4 metres across and 1 metre deep.* Here, *long* marks the primary, most extended, dimension, while *wide* and *deep* mark secondary dimensions. In general, children acquire terms for the positive, extended ends of spatial dimensions before they learn terms for the corresponding relative absence of extent.

This pattern of acquisition, it's been argued, is built on various perceptual and conceptual asymmetries, hence their universal status. For example, figures are more prominent perceptually than grounds in Gestalt terms, just as symmetrical figures are more salient than asymmetric ones. Children talk about figures before grounds, and learn terms for symmetric figures earlier. Both of these effects have a perceptual basis. A second example: children learn the words for single category members before they learn how to talk about several together. Here the singular is conceptually prior, and the plural is acquired only later. Virtually all languages add to singular terms in order to make them plural, as in English *cat* versus *cats*, or *house* versus *houses*. In general, children have spontaneous recourse to perceptual and conceptual patterns already established: they build on these as they look for meanings to map onto forms.

Languages differ in how much they depend on word order, on case marking, and on agreement to show what belongs with what in an utterance. They also differ in how finely they categorize some domains, and how many terms they make use of in doing so (e.g. terms for kinds of rice across different languages). Languages differ too in how they package the elements of meaning expressed in the lexicon – whether, for example, they combine motion with manner (as in *stroll, gallop*) or motion with direction (as in *enter, climb*) in verbs of motion. And they may also differ in how they express static location (*The books are on the shelf*) versus motion in space (*The kangaroo hopped onto the bank*).

One distinction researchers have drawn is that between the *semantic complexity* and the *formal complexity* of what's expressed in a language. While semantic complexity (based on underlying conceptual distinctions) should be much the same in children acquiring a first language, languages may differ a lot in formal complexity. Some rely on word order to convey grammatical relations like subject, verb, and object; others rely on case-marking instead. Some have an elaborate vocabulary for talking about position and motion, with different verbs depending on the properties of the object that is placed or moving, while others may have a very sparse vocabulary for this domain, with only one or two verbs of placement and motion that are put to use everywhere. In some languages, relative clauses may be particularly difficult to construct because they have to precede the nouns that they modify, while in others, relative clauses are easier, following directly after those nouns. The latter construction type is acquired earlier. In some languages, the plural is easy to express, with a small number of variants of a single ending added to nearly all nouns, as in English *pups*, *combs*, and *purses*; in others, the plural marker may vary with the noun class or group, and with case. It may also vary as function of picking out a set of individuals (e.g. *trees*) versus a collection (*forest*), and the plural ending may contrast with the dual (two things) and trial (three things) endings. In English, children have usually mastered conventional plural marking by age 3 to 4; but in Arabic it takes six to eight years longer, up to age 12, for children to master the full plural system.

Formal complexity, then, is one way languages differ in specific constructions and paradigms. And the paths children follow appear in large part to be a function of formal complexity. Semantic complexity, on the other hand, is assumed to be fairly comparable across languages, such that, regardless of language, children make the relevant conceptual distinctions at around the same age and stage in cognitive development. But to map the relevant semantic information as the meanings of specific forms itself may itself be complicated for young children, and this may make some semantic domains easier to master than others.

Conclusion

Language serves both social and conceptual goals from the start. Children are immersed in language because adults use it for talking with them about all that is going on. Children have to learn how to map language onto their world so that they can understand what adults are talking about when they comment on events and activities, when they negotiate over dressing, eating, or bath-time play, and when they tell or read stories.

Learning a first language depends on several factors: children must analyse the speech stream for patterns, in order to find words in the language and store them in memory; they need to keep track of any words they detect to find out what they probably mean and how to use them; they need to monitor what they themselves produce against any forms of language they have stored in memory; and when they detect mismatches between their own productions and target-forms stored in memory, they need to make repairs to change their own productions into a more recognizable form.

The general path that children follow in the course of acquisition reflects their gradual mapping of words to the perceptual and conceptual categories they draw on as they work to establish the meanings carried by specific terms and expressions. Both social and cognitive factors interact within each culture to shape the form/meaning relations children must master as they acquire a first language.

General resources and further reading

Reference books

(a) Extensive general overview and reference source, from an interactive point of view:

Clark, E. V. 2016. *First Language Acquisition* (3rd edn). Cambridge: Cambridge University Press.

(b) Focus on syntactic acquisition, from different theoretical perspectives in linguistics:

Ambridge, B., & Lieven, E. V. M. 2011. *Child Language Acquisition: Contrasting Theoretical Approaches*. Cambridge: Cambridge University Press.

(c) Focus on phonological acquisition:

Jusczyk, P. W. 2000. *The Discovery of Spoken Language*. Cambridge, MA: MIT Press.

Vihman, M. M. 2013. *Phonological Development: The First Two Years*. New York: John Wiley & Sons.

(d) Focus on meaning, in lexical and semantic acquisition:

Bloom, P. 2000. *How Children Learn the Meanings of Words*. Cambridge, MA: MIT Press.

Clark, E. V. 1993. *The Lexicon in Acquisition*. Cambridge: Cambridge University Press.

(e) Some useful handbooks:

Bavin, E. L., & Naigles, L. R. (Eds.). 2015. *Cambridge Handbook of Child Language* (2nd edn). Cambridge: Cambridge University Press.

Genesee, F., Paradis, J., & Crago, M.B. (Eds.). 2004. *Dual Language Development and Disorders: A Handbook on Bilingualism and Second Language Learning*. Baltimore, MD: Paul H. Brookes Publishing.

Hoff, E., & Shatz, M. (Eds.). 2009. *Blackwell Handbook of Language Development*. London: Wiley-Blackwell.

MacWhinney, B., & O'Grady, W. (Eds.). 2015. *The Handbook of Language Emergence.* London: Wiley-Blackwell.

Slobin, D. I. (Ed.), 1985–1997. *The Crosslinguistic Study of Language Acquisition* (5 vols.). Hillsdale, NJ: Lawrence Erlbaum.

(f) A useful general bibliography:

Clark, E. V., 2016. Acquisition of language. Oxford Bibliographies Online. http://www.oxfordbibliographies.com/view/document/obo-9780199772810/obo-9780199772810-0002.xml

Data sources

CHILDES Archive (Child Language Data Exchange System): transcribed recordings, some with video and/or audio, of children at different stages in language development, with data from a variety of languages.

For details on how to access and use this archive, and the languages represented there, see:

MacWhinney, B. 2000. *The CHILDES Project: Tools for Analyzing Talk* (3rd edn). Mahwah, NJ: Lawrence Erlbaum.

http://childes.psy.cmu.edu/

Further reading by chapter

Chapter 1: Where do children learn a first language?

Chouinard, M. M., & Clark, E. V. 2003. Adult reformulations of child errors as negative evidence. *Journal of Child Language* **30**, 637–669.

Clark, E. V. 2007. Young children's uptake of new words in conversation. *Language in Society* **36**, 157–182.

Clark, E. V. 2014. Pragmatics in acquisition. *Journal of Child Language* (40th anniversary issue, Supplement 1) **41**, 105–116.

Clark, E. V., & Estigarribia, B. 2011. Using speech and gesture to inform young children about unfamiliar word meanings. *Gesture* **11**, 1–23.

Clark, E. V., & Wong, A. D.-W. 2002. Pragmatic directions about language use: words and word meanings. *Language in Society* **31**, 181–212.

Fenson, L., Dale, P., Reznick, J. S., Bates, E., Thal, D. J., & Pethick, S. J. 1994. Variability in early communicative development. *Monographs of the Society for Research in Child Development* **54** (Serial No. 242).

Fletcher, P. 1985. *A Child's Learning of English*. Oxford: Basil Blackwell.

Greenfield, P. M., & Smith, J. H. 1976. *The Structure of Communication in Early Language Development*. New York: Academic Press.

Küntay, A., & Slobin, D. I. 1996. Listening to a Turkish mother: some puzzles for acquisition. In D. I. Slobin, J. Gerhardt, A. Kyratzis, & J. Guo (Eds.), *Social Interaction, Social Context, and Language: Essays in Honor of Susan Ervin Tripp* (pp. 265–296). Mahwah, NJ: Lawrence Erlbaum.

Olson, J., & Masur, E. F. 2011. Infants' gestures influence mothers' provision of object, action and internal state labels. *Journal of Child Language* **38**, 1028–1054.

Perra, O., & Gattis, M. (2012). Attention engagement in early infancy. *Infant Behavior and Development* **35**, 635–644.

Schieffelin, B. B. 1979. Getting it together: an ethnographic approach to the study of the development of communicative competence. In E. Ochs & B. B. Schieffelin (Eds.), *Developmental Pragmatics* (pp. 73–108). New York: Academic Press.

Scollon, R. 1976. *Conversations with a One Year Old*. Honolulu, HI: University of Hawai'i Press.

Shatz, M. 1979. How to do things by asking: form-function pairings in mothers' questions and their relation to children's responses. *Child Development* **50**, 1093–1099.

Snow, C. E. 1977. The development of conversation between mothers and babies. *Journal of Child Language* **4**, 1–22.

Snow, C. E., & Ferguson, C. A. (Eds.), 1974. *Talking to Children: Language Input and Acquisition*. Cambridge: Cambridge University Press.

Strapp, C. M. 1999. Mothers', fathers', and siblings' responses to children's language errors: comparing sources of negative evidence. *Journal of Child Language* **26**, 373–391.

Chapter 2: Recognizing and producing words

Berko, J., & Brown, R. 1960. Psycholinguistic research methods. In P. H. Mussen (Ed.), *Handbook of Research Methods in Child Development* (pp. 517–557). New York: John Wiley & Sons.

Casillas, M. A. 2014. Turn taking. In D. Matthews (Ed.), *Pragmatic Development* (pp. 53–70). Amsterdam: John Benjamins.

Clark, E. V., & Lindsey, K. L. 2015. Turn-taking: a case study of early gesture and word use in responses to WHERE and WHICH questions. *Frontiers in Psychology* **6**, article 890.

Dodd, B. 1975. Children's understanding of their own phonological forms. *Quarterly Journal of Experimental Psychology* **27**, 165–172.

Fernald, A., Perfors, A., & Marchman, V. A. 2006. Picking up speed in understanding: speech processing efficiency and vocabulary growth across the second year. *Developmental Psychology* **42**, 98–116.

Jakobson, R. 1968. *Child Language, Aphasia, and Phonological Universals*. The Hague: Mouton.

Jusczyk, P. W. 1997. *The Discovery of Spoken Language*. Cambridge, MA: MIT Press.

Kuhl, P. K., Conboy, B. T., Coffey-Corina, S., Padden, D., Rivera-Gaxiola, M., & Nelson, T. 2008. Phonetic learning as a pathway to language: new data and native language magnet theory expanded (NLM-e). *Philosophical Transactions of the Royal Society B* **363**, 979–1000.

Levelt, W. J. M. 1989. *Speaking: From Intention to Articulation*. Cambridge, MA: MIT Press.

Smith, N. V. 1973. *The Acquisition of Phonology: A Case Study*. Cambridge: Cambridge University Press.

Swingley, D., & Aslin, R. N. 2000. Spoken word recognition and lexical representation in very young children. *Cognition* **76**, 147–166.

Vihman, M. 1996. *Phonological Development: The Origins of Language in the Child*. Oxford: Blackwell.

Werker, J. F., & Lalonde, C. E. 1988. Cross-language speech perception: initial capabilities and developmental change. *Developmental Psychology* **24**, 672–683.

Chapter 3: Mapping meanings to words

Bates, E., Camaioni, L., & Volterra, V. 1975. The acquisition of performatives prior to speech. *Merrill-Palmer Quarterly* **21**, 205–226.

Bowerman, M., & Choi, S. 2003. Space under construction: language-specific spatial categorization in first language acquisition. In D. Gentner & S. Goldin-Meadow (Eds.), *Language in Mind* (pp. 387–427). Cambridge, MA: MIT Press.

Bruner, J. S. 1975. The ontogenesis of speech acts. *Journal of Child Language* **2**, 1–20.

Bloom, P. 2000. *How Children Learn the Meanings of Words*. Cambridge, MA: MIT Press.

Clark, E. V. 1973. Non-linguistic strategies and the acquisition of word meanings. *Cognition* **2**, 161–182.

Clark, E. V. 1993. *The Lexicon in Acquisition.* Cambridge: Cambridge University Press.

Clark, E. V. (2007). Young children's uptake of new words in conversation. *Language in Society* **36**, 157–182.

Clark, E. V., & Estigarribia, B. 2011. Using speech and gesture to inform young children about unfamiliar word meanings. *Gesture* **11**, 1–23.

Fenson, L., Dale, P. S., Reznick, J. S., Bates, E., Thal, D. J., & Pethick, S. J. 1994. Variability in early communicative development. *Monographs of the Society for Research in Child Development* **59** (serial no. 242).

Horst, J. S., Parsons, K. L., & Bryan, N. M. 2011. Get the story straight: contextual repetition promotes word learning from storybooks. *Frontiers in Psychology* **2**, article 17.

Horst, J. S., & Samuelson, L. K. 2008. Fast mapping but poor retention by 24-month-old infants. *Infancy* **13**, 128–157.

Matthews, D., Butcher, J., Lieven, E., & Tomasello, M. 2012. Two- and four-year-olds learn to adapt referring expressions to context: effects of distracters and feedback on referential communication. *Topics in Cognitive Science* **4**, 184–210.

Roy, B. C., Frank, M. C., and Roy, D. 2012. Relating activity contexts to early word learning in dense longitudinal data. *Proceedings of the 34th Annual Meeting of the Cognitive Science Society*, Sapporo, Japan.

Chapter 4: Using language

Bornstein, M., Putnick, D. L., Cote, L. R., Haynes, O. M., & Suwalsky, J. T. D. 2015. Mother-infant contingent vocalizations in 11 countries. *Psychological Science* **26**, 1272–1284.

Casillas, M. C. 2014. Taking the floor on time: delay and deferral in children's turn taking. In I. Arnon, M. Casillas, C. Kurumada, & B. Estigarribia (Eds.), *Language in Interaction: Studies in Honor of Eve V. Clark* (pp. 101–114). Amsterdam: John Benjamins.

Casillas, M. C., Bobb, S. B., & Clark, E. V. 2016. Turn taking, timing, and planning in early language acquisition. *Journal of Child Language* **43**, 000–000.

Chouinard, M. M., & Clark, E. V. 2003. Adult reformulations of child errors as negative evidence. *Journal of Child Language* **30**, 637–669.

Clark, E. V. 1987. The principle of contrast: a constraint on language acquisition. In B. MacWhinney (Ed.), *Mechanisms of Language Acquisition*
(pp. 1–33). Hillsdale, NJ: Lawrence Erlbaum.

Clark, E. V. 1990. On the pragmatics of contrast. *Journal of Child Language*
17, 417–431.

Clark, E. V. 1993. *The Lexicon in Acquisition*. Cambridge: Cambridge
University Press.

Clark, E. V. 2007. Young children's uptake of new words in conversation.
Language in Society **36**, 157–182.

Clark, E. V. 2010. Adult offer, word-class, and child uptake in early lexical
acquisition. *First Language* **30**, 250–269.

Clark, E. V. 2015. Common ground. In B. MacWhinney & W. O'Grady (Eds.), *The
Handbook of Language Emergence* (pp. 328–353). London: Wiley-Blackwell.

Clark, E. V., & Bernicot, J. 2008. Repetition as ratification: how parents and
children place information in common ground. *Journal of Child Language*
35, 349–371.

Clark, E. V., & Estigarribia, B. 2011. Using speech and gesture to introduce
new objects to young children. *Gesture* **11**, 1–23.

Clark, E. V., & Lindsey, K. L. 2015. Turn-taking: a case study of early gesture
and word use in answering WHERE and WHICH questions. *Frontiers in
Psychology* **6**, article 890.

Clark, H. H. 1996. *Using Language*. Cambridge: Cambridge University Press.

Flom, R., & Pick, A. D. 2003. Verbal encouragement and joint attention in
18-month-olds. *Infant Behavior and Development* **26**, 121–134.

Forrester, M. 2013. Mutual adaptation in parent-child interaction: learning
how to produce questions and answers. *Interaction Studies* **14**, 190–211.

Grice, H. P. 1989. *Studies in the Way of Words*. Cambridge, MA: Harvard
University Press.

Hillbrink, E. E., Gattis, M., & Levinson, S. C. 2015. Early developmental
changes in the timing of turn-taking: a longitudinal study of mother-infant
interaction. *Frontiers in Psychology* **6**, article 1492.

Karmiloff-Smith, A. 1981. The grammatical marking of thematic structure in
the development of language production. In W. Deutsch (Ed.), *The Child's
Construction of Language* (pp. 121–147). London: Academic Press.

Katsos, N., & Bishop, D. V. M. 2011. Pragmatic tolerance: implications for
the acquisition of informativeness and implicature. *Cognition* **120**, 67–81.

Papafragou, A., & Tantalou, N. 2004. The computation of implicatures by
young children. *Language Acquisition* **12**, 71–82.

Scollon, R. 1976. *Conversations with a One Year Old*. Honolulu, HI: University of Hawai'i Press.

Snow, C. E. 1978. The conversational context of language acquisition. In R. N. Campbell & P. T. Smith (Eds.), *Recent Advances in the Psychology of Language* (pp. 253–269). London: Plenum.

Stivers, T., Enfield, N. J., Brown, P., Englert, C., Hayashi, M., Heinemann, T., Hoymann, G., Rossano, F., de Ruiter, J.-P., Yoon, K.-E., & Levinson, S. C. 2009. Universals and cultural variation in turn-taking in conversation. *Proceedings of the National Academy of Sciences* **106,** 10587–10592.

Yurovsky, D., Smith, L. B., & Yu, C. Statistical word learning at scale: the baby's view is better. *Developmental Science* **16**, 959–966.

Chapter 5: Early constructions

Abbot-Smith, K., & Tomasello, M. 2006. Exemplar-learning and schematization in a usage-based account of syntactic acquisition. *The Linguistic Review* **23**, 275–290.

Antinucci, F., & Miller, R. 1976. How children talk about what happened. *Journal of Child Language* **3**, 167–189.

Arnon, I., & Clark, E. V. 2011. Why 'Brush your teeth' is better than 'Teeth': children's word production is facilitated in familiar sentence-frames. *Language Learning and Development* **7**, 107–129.

Bannard, C., & Matthews, D. 2008. Stored word sequences in language learning. *Psychological Science* **19**, 241–248.

Bloom, L., Lifter, K., & Hafitz, J. 1980. Semantics of verbs and the development of verb inflection in child language. *Language* **56**, 386–412.

Clark, E. V. 1996. Early verbs, event-types, and inflections. In C. E. Johnson & J. H. V. Gilbert (Eds.), *Children's Language*, vol. 9 (pp. 61–73). Mahwah, NJ: Erlbaum.

Clark, E. V., & de Marneffe, M.-C. 2012. Constructing verb paradigms in French: adult construals and emerging grammatical contrasts. *Morphology* **22**, 89–120.

Huttenlocher, J., Smiley, P., & Charney, R. 1983. Emergence of action categories in the child: evidence from verb meanings. *Psychological Review* **90**, 72–93.

Lieven, E., Pine, J. M., & Baldwin, G. 1997. Lexically-based learning and early grammatical development. *Journal of Child Language* **24**, 187–219.

Lieven, E., Salomo, D., & Tomasello, M. 2009. Two-year-old children's production of multiword utterances: a usage-based analysis. *Cognitive Linguistics* **20**, 481–507.

Messenger, K., Yuan, S., & Fisher, C. 2015. Learning verb syntax via listening: new evidence from 22-month-olds. *Language Learning and Development* **11**, 356–368.

Seva, N., Kempe, V., Brooks, P. J., Mironova, N., Pershukova, A., & Fedorova, O. 2007. Crosslinguistic evidence for the diminutive advantage: gender agreement in Russian and Serbian children. *Journal of Child Language* **34**, 111–131.

Slobin, D. I. (Ed.). 1985–1997. *The Crosslinguistic Study of Language Acquisition* (5 vols.). Hillsdale, NJ/Mahwah, NJ: Lawrence Erlbaum.

Smoczynska, M. 1985. The acquisition of Polish. In D. I. Slobin (Ed.), *The Crosslinguistic Study of Language Acquisition*, vol. 1 (pp. 595–686). Hillsdale, NJ: Lawrence Erlbaum.

Veneziano, E., & Clark, E. V. 2016. Early verb constructions in French: adjacency on the Left Edge. *Journal of Child Language* **43**, 000–000.

Chapter 6: More elaborate constructions

Ambridge, B., & Lieven, E. V. M. 2011. *Child Language Acquisition: Contrasting Theoretical Approaches*. Cambridge: Cambridge University Press.

Barner, D., Brooks, N., & Bale, A. 2011. Accessing the unsaid: the role of scalar alternatives in children's pragmatic inference. *Cognition* **118**, 84–93.

Bowerman, M. 1982. Evaluating competing linguistic models with language acquisition data: implications of developmental errors with causative verbs. *Quaderni di Semantici* **3**, 5–66.

Bowerman, M. 1986. First steps in acquiring conditionals. In E. C. Traugott, A. ter Meulen, J. S. Reilly, & C. A. Ferguson (Eds.), *On Conditionals* (pp. 285–307). Cambridge: Cambridge University Press.

Clark, E. V. 1971. On the acquisition of the meaning of before and after. *Journal of Verbal Learning and Verbal Behavior* **10**, 266–275.

Clark, E. V. 1982. The young word-maker: a case study of innovation in the child's lexicon. In E. Wanner & L. R. Gleitman (Eds.), *Language Acquisition: The State of the Art* (pp. 390–425). Cambridge: Cambridge University Press.

Clark, E. V., & Carpenter, K. L. 1989. The notion of source in language acquisition. *Language* **65**, 1–30.

Clark, E. V., & Nikitina, T. 2009. One vs. more than one: antecedents to plurality in early language acquisition. *Linguistics* **47**, 103–139.

Drozd, K. F. 1995. Child English pre-sentential negation as metalinguistic exclamatory sentence negation. *Journal of Child Language* **22**, 583–610.

Ervin-Tripp, S. 1970. Discourse agreement: how children answer questions. In J. R. Hayes (Ed.), *Cognition and the Development of Language* (pp. 79–107). New York: John Wiley & Sons.

Estigarribia, B. 2010. Facilitation by variation: right-to-left learning of English yes/no questions. *Cognitive Science* **34**, 68–93.

Goodman, J. C., McDonough, L., & Brown, N. B. 1998. The role of semantic context and memory in the acquisition of novel nouns. *Child Development* **69**, 1330–1344.

Johnson, C. E. 2000. What you see is what you get: the importance of transcription for interpreting children's morphosyntactic development. In L. Menn & N. Bernstein Ratner (Eds.), *Methods for Studying Language Production* (pp. 181–204). Mahwah, NJ: Lawrence Erlbaum.

Katsos, N., & Bishop, D. V. M. 2011. Pragmatic tolerance: implications for the acquisition of informativeness and implicature. *Cognition* **120**, 67–81.

Klima, E. S., & Bellugi, U. 1966. Syntactic regularities in the speech of children. In J. Lyons & R. J. Wales (Eds.), *Psycholinguistics Papers* (pp. 183–208). Edinburgh: University of Edinburgh Press.

Lakusta, L., & Landau, B. 2005. Starting at the end: the importance of goals in spatial language. *Cognition* **96**, 1–33.

Papafragou, A., & Skordos, D. 2016. Scalar implicature. In J. Lidz, W. Snyder, & J. Pater (Eds.), *The Oxford Handbook of Developmental Linguistics* (pp. 611–629). Oxford: Oxford.

Chapter 7: Carrying on a conversation

Andersen, E. S. 1990. *Speaking with Style: The Sociolinguistic Skills of Children*. London: Routledge.

Axia, G. 1996. How to persuade mum to buy a toy. *First Language* **16**, 301–317.

Bretherton, I. 1989. Pretense: the form and function of make-believe play. *Developmental Review* **9**, 383–401.

Casillas, M., Bobb, S. C., & Clark, E. V. 2016. Turn taking, timing, and planning in early language acquisition. *Journal of Child Language* **43**, 000–000.

Clark, E. V. 2015. Common ground. In B. MacWhinney & W. O'Grady (Eds.), *Handbook of Language Emergence* (pp. 328–353). London: Wiley-Blackwell.

Clark, E. V., & Lindsey, K. L. 2015. Turn-taking: a case study of early gesture and word use in answering WHERE and WHICH questions. *Frontiers in Psychology* **6**, article 890.

Dunn, J., & Dale, N. 1984. I a daddy: two-year-olds' collaboration in joint pretend play with sibling and with mother. In I. Bretherton (Ed.), *Symbolic play: The Development of Social Understanding* (pp. 131–158). New York: Academic Press.

Ervin-Tripp, S. 1979. Children's verbal turn-taking. In E. Ochs & B. B. Schieffelin (Eds.), *Developmental Pragmatics* (pp. 391–414). New York: Academic Press.

Garvey, C., & Kramer, T. L. 1989. The language of social pretend play. *Developmental Review* **9**, 364–382.

Kaper, W. 1980. The use of the past tense in games of pretend. *Journal of Child Language* **7**, 213–215.

Lammertink, I., Casillas, M., Benders, T., Post, B., & Fikkert, P. 2015. Dutch and English toddlers' use of linguistic cues in predicting upcoming turn transitions. *Frontiers in Psychology* **6**, article 495.

Martlew, M., Connolly, K., & McCleod, C. 1978. Language use, role, and context in a five-year-old. *Journal of Child Language* **5**, 81–99.

Reed, B. K., & Cherry, L. J. 1978. Preschool children's production of directive forms. *Discourse Processes* **1**, 233–245.

Sachs, J., & Devin, J. 1976. Young children's use of age-appropriate speech styles in social interaction and role playing. *Journal of Child Language* **3**, 81–98.

Sawyer, R. K. 1997. *Pretend Play as Improvisation*. Mahwah, NJ: Lawrence Erlbaum.

Scollon, R. 1976. *Conversations with a One Year Old*. Honolulu, HI: University of Hawai'i Press.

Chapter 8: Perspectives, viewpoints, and voices

Andersen, E. S. 1990. *Speaking with Style: The Sociolinguistic Skills of Children*. London: Routledge.

Berman, R. A., & Slobin, D. I. 1994. *Relating Events in Narrative: A Crosslinguistic Developmental Study*. Hillsdale, NJ: Lawrence Erlbaum.

Callanan, M. A., & Sabbagh, M. A. 2004. Multiple labels for objects in conversations with young children: parents' language and children's developing expectations about word meanings. *Developmental Psychology* **40**, 746–763.

Chandler, M. J., Fritz, A. S., & Hala, S. M. 1989. Small-scale deceit: deception as a marker of two-, three- and four-years-olds' early theories of mind. *Child Development* **60**, 1263–1277.

Clark, E. V. 1997. Conceptual perspective and lexical choice in acquisition. *Cognition* **64**, 1–37.

Clark. E. V., & Grossman, J. B. 1998. Pragmatic directions and children's word learning. *Journal of Child Language* **25**, 1–18.

Clark, E. V., & Svaib, T. A. 1997. Speaker perspective and reference in young children. *First Language* **17**, 57–74.

Ferguson, H. J., Apperly, I., Ahmad, J., Bindemann, M., & Cane, J. 2015. Task constraints distinguish perspective inferences from perspective use during discourse interpretation in a false belief task. *Cognition* **139**, 50–70.

Garvey, C. 1975. Requests and responses in children's speech. *Journal of Child Language* **2**, 41–63.

Hoicka, E., & Akhtar, N. 2012. Early humour production. *British Journal of Developmental Psychology* **30**, 586–603.

Nardy, A., Chevrot, J.-P., & Barbu, S. 2014. Sociolinguistic convergence and social interactions within a group of preschoolers: a longitudinal study. *Language Variation and Change* **26**, 273–301.

O'Neill, D. K. 1996. Two-year-old children's sensitivity to a parent's knowledge state when making requests. *Child Development* **67**, 659–677.

Rubio-Fernández, P., & Geurts, B. How to pass the false-belief task before your fourth birthday. *Psychological Science* **24**, 27–33.

Sawyer, R. K. 1997. *Pretend Play as Improvisation*. Mahwah, NJ: Lawrence Erlbaum.

Shatz, M., & Gelman, R. 1973. The development of communication skills: modifications in the speech of young children as a function of listener. *Monographs of the Society for Research in Child Development*, vol. **38** [serial no. 152].

Slobin, D. I. 2014. From speech to others to speech for self: a case study of 'externalized drama'. In I. Arnon, M. Casillas, C. Kurumada, & B. Estigarribia (Eds.), *Language in Interaction: Studies in Honor of Eve V. Clark* (pp. 315–331). Amsterdam: John Benjamins.

Weissenborn, J. 1986. Learning how to become an interlocutor: the verbal negotiation of common frames of reference and actions in dyads of seven- to fourteen-year-old children. In J. Cook-Gumperz, W. A. Corsaro, & J. Streek (Eds.), *Children's Worlds and Children's Language* (pp. 377–404). Berlin: De Gruyter.

Chapter 9: More than one language at once

Bialystok, E. 2001. *Bilingualism in Development: Language, Literacy, and Cognition*. Cambridge: Cambridge University Press.

Catone, K. F. 2007. *Code-switching in Bilingual Children*. Dordrecht: Springer.

Cenoz, J., & Genesee, F. (Eds.). 2001. *Trends in Bilingual Acquisition*. Amsterdam: John Benjamins.

De Houwer, A. 2009. *Bilingual First Language Acquisition*. Bristol: Multilingual Matters.

De Houwer, A., Bornstein, M., & Putnick, D. 2014. A bilingual-monolingual comparison of young children's vocabulary size: evidence from comprehension and production. *Applied Psycholinguistics* **35**, 1189–1211.

Genesee, F., & Nicoladis, E. 2007. Bilingual first language acquisition. In E. Hoff & M. Shatz (Eds.), *Handbook of Language Development* (pp.324–342). Oxford: Blackwell.

Grosjean, F. 1982. *Life with Two Languages: An Introduction to Bilingualism*. Cambridge, MA: Harvard University Press.

Grüter, T., & Paradis, J. (Eds.). 2014. *Input and Experience in Bilingual Development*. Amsterdam: John Benjamins.

Hakuta, K. 1986. *Mirror of Language: The Debate on Bilingualism*. New York: Basic Books.

Jisa, H. 2000. Language mixing in the weak language: evidence from two children. *Journal of Pragmatics* **32**, 11363–1386.

Lanza, E. 2004. *Language Mixing in Infant Bilingualism: A Sociolinguistic Perspective*. Oxford: Oxford University Press.

Taeschner, T. 2012. *The Sun Is Feminine* (first published 1983). Berlin: Springer.

Weber, J.-J., & Horner, K. 2013. *Introducing Multilingualism: A Social Approach*. London: Routledge.

Yip, V., & Matthews, S. 2007. *The Bilingual Child: Early Development and Language Contact*. Cambridge: Cambridge University Press.

Chapter 10: Process in acquisition

Bowerman, M. 2012. *Ten Lectures on Language, Cognition, and Language Acquisition*. Beijing: Foreign Language Teaching & Research Press.

Chouinard, M. M., & Clark, E. V. 2003. Adult reformulations of child errors as negative evidence. *Journal of Child Language* **30**, 637–669.

Clark, E. V. 2001. Emergent categories in first language acquisition. In M. Bowerman & S. C. Levinson (Eds.), *Language Acquisition and Conceptual Development* (pp. 379–405). Cambridge: Cambridge University Press.

Clark, E. V. 2003. Languages and representations. In D. Gentner & S. Goldin-Meadow (Eds.), *Language in Mind* (pp. 17–24). Cambridge, MA: MIT.

Clark, E. V. 2016. *First Language Acquisition* (3rd edition). Cambridge: Cambridge University Press.

Clark, E. V., & Hecht, B. F. 1983. Comprehension, production, and language acquisition. *Annual Review of Psychology* **34**, 325–349.

Clark, E. V., & de Marneffe, M.-C. 2012. Constructing verb paradigms in French: adult construals and emerging grammatical contrasts. *Morphology* **22**, 89–120.

Clark, H. H. 1996. *Using Language*. Cambridge: Cambridge University Press.

Enfield, N. J., & Levinson, S. C. 2006. *Roots of Human Sociality*. New York: Berg.

Greenberg, J. H. 1966. *Language Universals*. Amsterdam: Mouton.

Karmiloff-Smith, A. 1998. Development itself is the key to understanding developmental disorders. *Trends in Cognitive Sciences* **2**, 389–398.

Levelt, W. J. M. 1989. *Speaking: From Intention to Articulation*. Cambridge, MA: MIT Press.

Moravcsik, E. A. 2013. *Introducing Language Typology*. Cambridge: Cambridge University Press.

Ortega, L. 2014. *Understanding Second Language Acquisition*. London: Routledge.

Slobin, D. S. (Ed.), 1985–1997. *The Crosslinguistic Study of Language Acquisition* (5 vols.). Hillsdale, NJ/Mahwah, NJ: Lawrence Erlbaum.

Subject index

Printed in Great
Britain
by Amazon